Early Childhood Leadership and Program Management

Other Redleaf Press Books by Angèle Sancho Passe

Creating Diversity-Rich Environments for Young Children

Dual-Language Learners: Strategies for Teaching English

Evaluating and Supporting Early Childhood Teachers

Is Everybody Ready for Kindergarten?

Redleaf *Quick* Guide

Early Childhood Leadership and Program Management

Angèle Sancho Passe

Redleaf Press®
www.redleafpress.org
800-423-8309

To all early education leaders who manage their program with care and skill.

Published by Redleaf Press
10 Yorkton Court
St. Paul, MN 55117
www.redleafpress.org

First edition 2022
Senior editor: Melissa York
Cover design by Renee Hammes
Cover photos by Monkey Business / dglimages / Rawpixel.com / stock.adobe.com
Typeset in Signo and Avenir by Douglas Schmitz
Printed in the United States of America
29 28 27 26 25 24 23 22   1 2 3 4 5 6 7 8

Library of Congress Cataloging-in-Publication Data

Names: Passe, Angèle Sancho, author.
Title: Early childhood leadership and program management / Angèle Sancho
  Passe.
Description: First edition. | St. Paul, MN : Redleaf Press, 2022. |
  Includes bibliographical references. | Summary: "Leading and managing an
  early education program is both challenging and rewarding. This book
  gives practical tips on running a child care program that boosts the
  confidence of new directors. It draws on the skills they already have,
  proposes strategies that focus on quality for teaching and learning, and
  organizational planning. It also addresses how to infuse a
  diversity-rich mindset to create successful environments for all staff,
  families, and children"-- Provided by publisher.
Identifiers: LCCN 2022000855 (print) | LCCN 2022000856 (ebook) | ISBN
  9781605547657 (paperback) | ISBN 9781605547664 (ebook)
Subjects: LCSH: Early childhood education--Administration. | Educational
  leadership.
Classification: LCC LB2822.6 .P37 2022 (print) | LCC LB2822.6 (ebook) |
  DDC 372.12--dc23/eng/20220314
LC record available at https://lccn.loc.gov/2022000855
LC ebook record available at https://lccn.loc.gov/2022000856

Printed on acid-free paper

CONTENTS

INTRODUCTION

Melinda likes being a center director. She feels organized and confident. Her staff is productive and collaborative. Families are loyal and trust that their children are getting good care and education. The children's assessments and behaviors show that they are learning well. In the state quality rating system, the program has a solid five stars. But this wasn't always the case. When she became the director, Melinda started out with high hopes but soon found herself overwhelmed with daily demands for time and patience that she had not anticipated. She was at work from dawn to late at night trying to solve every problem, with no end in sight, wondering what was wrong with herself and her staff. Near burnout, she decided that her positive vision could still happen, but only if she had a more systematic approach. After some research, she found that the field of early childhood education has useful tools, supportive organizations, and training courses to help her be a successful leader and manager. In one such class, she discovered the idea that she could put her skills as a teacher to use in her job as a director.

Leading and managing an early education program is both challenging and rewarding. Often education leaders start as teachers and are later selected or self-identified as leaders. This means that as teachers-turned-leaders, they have a toolbox of techniques they already know to lead their program. However, leaders do not always recognize this parallel.

We expect early educators to reflect on their practice so they can meet the needs of children. It's important for education leaders to reflect too. In my work with programs, I observe that managers, directors, or principals often focus their attention on children's learning more than on the staff. They want the children to do well, but they bypass the medium by which children learn: the educators themselves and the system in which they work. If the ultimate goal is the success of children, it follows that the leader's first goal should be the well-being and functioning of the people who make that possible—the staff who work directly with children. And for that to happen, the center's daily operations must be well run and efficient.

This Quick Guide on early childhood leadership and program management gives practical tips for running an early childhood program that boosts the confidence of directors so they can enjoy the rewards of making a positive impact on children, families, and staff. It draws on the techniques they already know and the skills they already have to do a good job. It proposes strategies that focus on quality for teaching and learning, as well as organizational planning and strength. It addresses how to view the job with a diversity and equity lens to create inclusive environments for all staff, families, and children.

Leader or Manager?

Some thinkers separate the two roles of leader and manager. The leader inspires workers to perform. The manager enforces rules and policies to get workers to perform. This separation of functions may be possible in large organizations that can afford big administration teams. In early childhood education (ECE), programs are usually run on lean budgets that limit the number of administrators. You have to be both leader and manager and make it work. You can succeed because you have the characteristics of a teacher—especially when you use the skills that made you a successful teacher. Managers organize people, while leaders motivate them. Teachers do the same thing. They organize their classrooms with schedules, transitions, and routines. They introduce interesting and engaging activities to inspire the children to learn. They provide a calm physical and social environment to motivate the children to get along and grow in all areas of development. Rather than "classroom management," good teachers provide "behavior guidance." They pay attention to people in addition to processes and procedures. In a well-run classroom, children know what to do, they show appropriate behavior, and they learn social and academic skills. Even though it might look easy to observers, we know the success is due to the efforts of the teacher. Running a program is very similar.

The objectives of this book are the following:

- to examine the role of the education leader

- to present practical strategies to use in your daily work of managing a program

- to recognize the expertise you already have, so you increase your confidence

- to help you make a personal plan that you can follow as you continue to grow in your skills

Each chapter is organized to help you think about the parallels between the job of teachers and leaders and to view each topic with a diversity and equity lens.

Guiding you to make a plan is a principal aim of this book. At the end of each chapter, you will find a reflection and planning section to help you be specific in identifying your strengths, recognizing your areas to improve, and recording your next goals. As you read, record the ideas you already know and strategies you already use. Take a moment to congratulate yourself. You have a solid foundation for your next steps. Then focus on new ideas and strategies that would make your work more effective. Ultimately, your effectiveness will result in a most satisfying professional experience.

SMART Goals

Your goals should be SMART (Specific, Measurable, Achievable, Relevant, and Time-bound). For example:

Goal: Improve maintenance of outdoor equipment (slides, riding toys, climbers) to increase safety of children as they play.

Specific—What is the specific idea? Who will do it?

I will set up a schedule and process and engage the staff to inspect and maintain the outdoor equipment to ensure safety and to improve our rating from the licensing office.

Measurable—How will you measure success?

Accidents due to equipment in disrepair will be eliminated. Broken equipment will be taken out of the playground to be fully repaired or replaced.

Achievable—Is it possible to achieve with the resources you have?

I will conduct inspections myself twice a week. In addition, I will find or design a simple checklist for each teacher to report problems every day as they are outside supervising children's play.

Relevant—Will it benefit your particular situation?

Very relevant. A system for maintenance must be put in place because the program is in violation of licensing rules, and having accidents (even minor ones) due to broken equipment is unacceptable for children. We received a warning from the licensor after the last observation.

Time-bound—By when will it happen?

We will start this system of inspection and maintenance on Monday and continue indefinitely. I will keep a weekly record for the center. We will be ready for the next inspection by the licensing office in three months.

Competencies and Dispositions

In this book, you will find many examples and suggestions that will help you rediscover and put into practice the competencies and dispositions you already have. In the process of developing core competencies for early educators in Minnesota, a task force held conversations with many groups that were diverse in terms of geographic location, culture, and type of program. In the resulting document, *Minnesota's Knowledge and Competency Framework for Early Childhood Professionals*, they identified a set of dispositions that were common across all the groups (Minnesota Departments of Education, Human Services, and Health 2020).

An early educator . . .

- is compassionate and sensitive.

- has a sense of humor.

- is curious and open to new ideas.

- can be flexible and resourceful.

- asks questions and demonstrates an interest in learning.

- reflects on current practices to improve them.

- likes children and believes in their ability to learn.

- is optimistic when faced with challenges.

- is collaborative.

- shows respect for self and others.

- values and appreciates differences.

- demonstrates a high level of integrity.

This list is complemented with these general work habits. An early educator . . .

- is punctual and responsible.

- cares for personal hygiene and dresses appropriately for the activity.

- expects and responds flexibly to continuous change.

- accepts constructive feedback and learns from mistakes.

- listens and responds appropriately.

The document talks of these dispositions as skills that may be mostly innate. But I propose that all of them can be learned because they are so essential to success. As you read the list, reflect on how these dispositions also fit the role of an education leader. I hope you recognize yourself as you see the parallel between the work of an educator and that of an education leader. There is no reason you cannot apply these characteristics to the job of director.

Right now these skills and dispositions may feel buried under the daily tasks of running a program or a center. As a leader, you have to provide for the needs of children and families, plus you have to consider all members of your staff (teaching and nonteaching), the finances, the building, and the community. It's a big job. Take heart. I invite you to reflect on and unearth your knowledge, skills, and dispositions, then examine how to practice them in the various situations you face.

Useful Resources and Philosophies

There is a solid body of research and best practices to help education leaders do a good job of leading and managing programs, dealing with organizational matters as well as keeping an anti-bias and inclusive perspective. Institutions like the National Association for the Education of Young Children (NAEYC), the McCormick Center for Early Childhood Leadership, and First Children's Finance provide information and resources. Frameworks and tools that many leaders find helpful in their work include *Anti-Bias Education for Young Children and Ourselves* (Derman-Sparks and Olsen Edwards 2020), *Skilled Dialogue* (Barrera and Kramer 2017), and the Pyramid Model (www.pyramidmodel.org), to which I would add my own writing: *Evaluating and Supporting Early Childhood Teachers* (Passe 2015) and *Creating Diversity-Rich Environments for Young Children* (Passe 2020). These books focus on the topics of leadership and management, too, if you are interested in more in-depth exploration.

The NAEYC Code of Ethical Conduct (NAEYC 2011) places the welfare and safety of children above all other obligations. It also clearly states responsibilities toward staff, such as respecting human dignity, promoting professional satisfaction, and modeling positive relationships. The education leader is expected to create and promote conditions of trust, cooperation, well-being, confidentiality, growth, and self-esteem, just as teachers are expected to promote and implement these values in their classrooms.

The NAEYC position statement on diversity and equity (NAEYC 2019) expects teachers to uphold the unique value and dignity of each child; involve children in the design and implementation of learning; recognize and be prepared to provide different levels of support; and consider how their own biases may be contributing to negative messages or interactions with children and families. That applies well to the work of leaders with their staff. Education leaders must uphold the unique value of each staff member; involve staff in the running of the program; offer different levels of support; and consider their own biases when leading their program. Cultural identity is complex, and we must view diversity with many dimensions because there is not just one way people think of themselves. Many factors describe who we are, like age, education, ethnicity, family constellation, gender, home-geographic roots, language, mental ability, nationality, neurodiversity, occupation, physical ability, race, religion, sexual orientation, and socioeconomic status.

The 2020 version of the NAEYC position statement on developmentally appropriate practice (NAEYC 2020) for teaching of children has some particular points that are worth applying to the work of leaders, especially the notion of a curriculum that offers both mirrors and windows, where children's lives and experiences are reflected and where new ideas are presented to enlarge their knowledge of the world. The same goes for the work of leaders with staff. As a mirror, you offer to your staff a reflection of the work they do. You offer affirmations and feedback to help them be confident and effective. As a window, you propose new ideas and practices and offer training and coaching to help them grow and keep up the quality of your program.

The work of the McCormick Center for Early Childhood Leadership (https://mccormickcenter.nl.edu) divides the role of the education leader into three aspects: pedagogical leadership, administrative leadership, and leadership essentials. The parallels with teaching include coaching and mentoring; applying knowledge of development to learning; using knowledge of assessment and ability to interpret data; planning strategically, based on results; having awareness of organizational climate; having awareness of self and others; acting with intentionality; applying knowledge of the profession; utilizing communication and team-building skills; demonstrating cultural competence; and acting according to ethical standards and morality.

First Children's Finance (www.firstchildrensfinance.org) supports the needs of child care centers and leaders with resources for building financial and business skills. It offers trainings, consulting, and many practical tools on budgeting, record keeping, enrollment, marketing, facilities, governance, and other necessary tasks of leading and managing a program.

Leading Anti-Bias Early Childhood Programs: A Guide for Change, **by Louise Derman-Sparks and her colleagues** (2015), informs the leader's role in building anti-bias early childhood programs. It acknowledges that anti-bias education is "messy work." It also engages leaders in seeing diversity as an asset to the organization and provides concrete ways to think about equity and make it happen every day. The same principles are embedded in the NAEYC position statement *Advancing Equity in Early Childhood Education* (2019).

The Pyramid Model (www.pyramidmodel.org) posits that children need a gradated approach with guidance to learn social-emotional competence. At the base of the pyramid, all children build relationships in supportive environments that promote positive social learning. Then, going up higher on the pyramid, some children need extra teaching support to learn specific social-emotional skills. Finally, at the top of the pyramid, a small group of children need even more support, in the form of individualized interventions. The same concept applies to adults. According to the field of human resource development, problems in the workplace environment usually relate to interpersonal conflict, miscommunication, or poor decision-making (Bloom et. al. 2016). When leaders understand this idea, they can use the pyramid model in their work with staff and families. All adults need a responsive environment that promotes positive relationships, just as children do. A smaller group of adults needs extra support, and some individuals need targeted interventions. That is the everyday work of leaders of an early childhood program. When children—or staff or family members—are experiencing anger, stress, sadness, or frustration and exhibit challenging behavior, it is important for the leader to be the voice of reason and to stay calm. The goal is to provide the safety and support they need as they learn to regroup and move on.

The model of *skilled dialogue* presented by Isaura Barrera and Lucinda Kramer (2017) is an approach that honors cultural beliefs and values. For educators, it means valuing the experiences of children and families and using them as the foundation for learning new ways. This concept also relates to the work of education leaders with their staff and family members. The practice promotes respectful and responsive interactions. It reframes differences as complementary rather than contradictory.

In *Evaluating and Supporting Early Childhood Teachers*, I define *evaluation* as a way to "find the value of" and *support* as a way to "uphold, stand by, and provide for" (Passe 2015, 8). With these positive images, education leaders can address quality of teaching with three aspects: the acts of teaching (what the teacher does directly with the children); the results of teaching (what children learn as the result of the acts of teaching); and professional behaviors (behaviors that make a teacher a good worker).

Creating Diversity-Rich Environments for Young Children (Passe 2020) provides guidance for early childhood professionals in creating a positive and inclusive program for children, families, and staff of all cultures, backgrounds, and experiences. It helps educators and leaders infuse the principles of diversity and equity into all aspects of early childhood education.

CHAPTER 1
THE ROLE OF THE
EDUCATION LEADER

Sally was a very competent lead teacher. She was recently promoted to director of a child care center and was excited about her new job. But a little while into it, the joy was gone, replaced by a nagging crisis of self-confidence. Some of the staff openly resisted her ideas for change. She sensed tension in the teachers' lounge. The new curriculum was not being used. The finances were not as positive as they could be. Sally questioned her ability to manage the program and wondered if she had what it takes. Fortunately, she could find resources. She joined a directors' group sponsored by her state Association for the Education of Young Children (AEYC). She took an online class on evaluating and supporting early educators. She reached out to a former director, who pointed out to her that she already had many of the skills she needed to lead and manage, especially from her experience as a successful toddler teacher. She used to call teaching the little ones "organizing chaos"—exactly the situation she was in now. With a new smile on her face and a plan for organizing the present chaos, Sally regained her confidence.

Parallels between Teaching and Leading

In a quality classroom, teachers intentionally arrange the environment to support children in getting along and playing together. They establish routines, have enough toys to share, and remind the children of the rules of behavior. The message is "We're all in this together." Education leaders can have the same message for their staff. They do that with caring behavior, fair working conditions, professional resources, positive and constructive feedback, empathetic direction, and clear communication. Their message is "Even though some days are challenging, you can count on me to support you in doing a good job."

Important Considerations

As a leader, you are accountable for quality in teaching and learning, as well as in the running of the food program, the condition of the space, the budget, and so on. The McCormick Center for Early Childhood Leadership conducted a study (McCormick Center 2011) to assess how the overall quality of centers fared when directors received mentoring. The results showed that programs improved in all areas, including in the way the teachers interacted with children. It was particularly interesting that the project found an increase in teacher sensitivity and a decrease in harshness. This proves the point of the parallel process: treat the staff well, as we want them to treat children, and they in turn treat the children well.

- Leaders are decision makers. They make thousands of decisions a day; some are routine, and others are emergencies. Sometimes the decision is based on previous experience, such as when they need to find a sub for an absent teacher and they already have a system for handling this situation. Other times it is a new situation, such as when the refrigerator breaks down and the cook has just received the food order for the week.

- Leaders are team builders. They are responsible for creating a community of workers who can get things done. They help their staff resolve conflicts and solve problems. Their job is to facilitate a climate that promotes care, creativity, and competence. They mobilize strangers of varying competencies to coordinate their skills to care for and teach children. They build and coach individual workers into a professional community.

- Leaders are change agents. They have the overall picture for the program that they must share with their team. They introduce new ideas, such as a new curriculum or new materials, or they reassign staff according to their skills or the needs of the center.

- Leaders create and maintain a positive environment. This shines through both with big decisions and with little daily acts, such as smiling and greetings. They affirm their staff's good work, and they support them during challenging times. As they guide, they cannot be bossy.

- Leaders must have the equivalent of a lesson plan that maps the day, week, and year of their program. They provide direction for all aspects of the program: pedagogy (curriculum, teaching, and family engagement), administration (planning, workplace climate, finances, staffing, and space and equipment), and professionalism (empathy, respect, adaptability, and ethics).

Practical Applications

Apply a Diversity and Equity Lens to the Role of Education Leader

Program leaders are responsible for utilizing the resources listed in the introduction. They set the tone in ensuring that all children, families, and staff members see themselves and others represented in the program. That happens in everyday actions of hiring, purchasing materials, implementing curriculum, designing staff development, and facilitating meetings. They lead a program where differences are managed respectfully and where everyone is welcome, not only in words but in daily experiences. They must be alert, aware, and intentional about diversity at all times. Their compass is the principles found in *Anti-Bias Education for Young Children and Ourselves* (Derman-Sparks and Olsen Edwards 2020) and in the position statement *Advancing Equity in Early Childhood Education* (NAEYC 2019).

Strategies for Being an Effective Leader

1. Focus on the staff. This requires intentionality, especially if you have left the classroom recently and are still drawn to the children. Remember that the staff are now your primary responsibility. Their welfare is your main concern, so they are free to do their job of caring for and teaching children.

2. Share your vision for quality with staff and families. That means presenting your ideas and listening to theirs. It can only make the vision stronger.

3. Provide clear direction. As the leader who plans for the program, you have the most knowledge of the future. For example, if you receive a new grant for playground equipment, let your teachers know when and how they will be involved in planning, what will be possible, and what is nonnegotiable. That eliminates the stress of surprises and speculation.

4. Empower your staff through a combination of direction, support, and autonomy. *Direction* is setting expectations for what needs to happen, such as saying the teacher must read a book at circle time every day. *Support* is giving the tools to do the task, such as providing a good library of children's books. *Autonomy* is letting the teacher choose which book to read. In this example, an experienced teacher might do well with a higher level of autonomy than a novice teacher. A novice teacher might need more support in choosing appropriate books. In that case, you would check in more often with the less-experienced teacher to support their skill acquisition until their confidence grows. In the field of organization development, it is known that employees feel empowered when they receive direction, support, and autonomy, calibrated to individuals.

5. Hire with intention. Hiring is the most important step in building your team. It can be challenging in our field and in times of low unemployment. In addition to the résumé, interview, and recommendations, consider having the person spend an hour in the classroom to observe their rapport with children and other staff.

6. Provide careful onboarding. Have a comprehensive employee manual that details the expectations and responsibilities of employees and employer. Discuss it with the new employee so you can point to the most critical elements you want to stress.

7. Promote a positive climate so you can retain and grow your team. In addition to paying fair wages based on rates in your area, pay attention to the other factors that influence retention, such as fairness in scheduling and treatment, a positive and gossip-free climate, and clear expectations.

8. Be visible. Stand at the door to greet families or to say goodbye. Walk the hallways and visit classrooms and the playground every day at different times. Make these interactions pleasant, with smiles and encouraging comments.

9. Be collaborative. Share your thinking with staff so they can understand the goals and work with you as a team. Involve your staff in setting a common agenda, not just for the big picture of early childhood education but for the details of your daily work, such as how to serve meals or the frequency of read-alouds. In that way, you also model a culture of collaboration.

10. Develop professional relationships with your staff. The word *relationships* can be misunderstood as becoming personal friends and creating a bond through happy hours or exchanging holiday gifts. In the professional setting of your center, it is preferable to build the bond through the vision that you and your team have for the children and families. Your common accomplishments are the strength of your connection. In the end, great personal friendships can grow out of shared profes-sional passion.

Reflection and Planning

As you finish reading this chapter, reflect on yourself as a leader and manager.

1. Which ideas are familiar, and which are you already using in your daily work?

2. Which ideas would you like to explore further?

3. Choose one or two ideas that you would like to focus on, and use the SMART goal-setting formula to write down your goal:

Specific (What is the specific idea? Who will do it?)	
Measurable (How will you measure success?)	
Achievable (Is it possible to accomplish with the resources you have?)	
Relevant (Will it benefit your particular situation?)	
Time-bound (By when will it happen?)	

CHAPTER 2
ADMINISTERING THE PROGRAM

When Sam went from the classroom to the office, she was a bit surprised. She had imagined herself as a pedagogical leader, supporting her staff in deepening their understanding of developmentally appropriate practice and coaching for quality teaching and learning. Instead, her first days were taken up with revising the budget and finding that records were incomplete; one staff member quit and another requested a part-time assignment for family reasons; the old dishwasher stopped working; and the board asked for an overdue report on the marketing and enrollment strategy. The situation was discouraging, yet she had no choice but to tackle these program administration matters. She found help at the monthly directors' coffee hour held at a local café. Some of her more experienced colleagues recommended that she set up systems for the different areas of program administration. They gave her good tips. She purchased a child care management solutions software package that made it easier to track enrollment, staffing, maintenance, and marketing. Within three months, the most urgent administrative tasks were under control, and she was feeling more competent as an administrative leader. Now she could broaden her attention to the pedagogical aspect of her job.

Parallels between Teaching and Leading

Teachers are responsible for caring and teaching. That includes health and safety issues as well as instructional issues. They must pay attention to the condition of toys, materials, and equipment that children use every day. They must have procedures for scheduling learning activities and for assessing children's learning, such as observation, documentation, and planning. Directors don't have direct responsibility for caring and educating children, but they use the same skills at a larger, systemic scale for the entire center: planning, scheduling, observing, assessing, documenting, and evaluating.

Important Considerations

For a director, administration consists of a number of focused management tasks and considerations. The *Program Administration Scale (PAS)* (Talan and Bloom 2011) lists these categories with some examples:

- Human resources development: orientation, development, supervision, and support of staff

- Personnel cost and allocation: salary scale, benefits, paid planning time

- Center operations: health and safety, risk management, staff meetings, internal communication

- Child assessment: availability and quality of assessment and screening

- Fiscal management: annual budget planning, payroll, expenses

- Program planning and evaluation: mission and vision statement, planning capacity

- Family partnerships: type and frequency of communication with families, support for families' needs, such as a resource library, scholarships, or referral services

- Marketing and public relations: type and frequency of external communication tools, effectiveness of administrator's community involvement, including membership in professional organizations and area business associations, connections to local elementary schools, and so on

- Technology: software and hardware, internet access

- Staff qualifications: levels of education, training, job experience of staff

Often education leaders claim these areas are not their favorite parts of the job. Frequently these areas of the work pop up as a surprise, like for Sam in the story. Sometimes planning seems like extra work. Yet attending to these considerations and planning for them does improve the systems of running a program, and planning is a good investment for leaders because it saves time, energy, and aggravation in the long run. Use the same strategies you used as a teacher planning for your classroom. Lesson planning prompts teachers to think about what the children need to learn ahead of time and accordingly plan what to teach. They prepare the schedule, space, activities, and materials. They anticipate contingencies such as rain. They also think about the characteristics of different children, such as their temperaments or interests. They realize that they still have to be flexible and adjust, but they also know that the day goes better when they have taken the time to plan. With a solid strategic plan, leaders avoid problems and face fewer emergencies. And in the end, this efficiency makes their job more effective and enjoyable.

Practical Applications

Apply a Diversity and Equity Lens to Program Administration

Program leaders are responsible for administering their program in a way that is fair for all children, families, and staff. Commitment to equitable experiences and outcomes must be reflected in all areas of operations: budget, equipment, use of time, levels of professional development support, and materials. It may mean budgeting for extra staff meeting time to make sure everyone has the opportunity to hear about a new policy and understand it; intentionally choosing books to reflect the diversity of families in the center; or providing individual coaching for teachers in culturally appropriate behavior guidance strategies.

Strategies for Effective Program Administration

1. Take full advantage of the technical resources available, both in your community and nationally. Find your local chapter of the National Association for the Education of Young Children (NAEYC) or a more informal network of directors in your area. First Children's Finance provides specialized business consulting for the child care field with information on all areas of management: marketing, finance, quality staffing, planning, evaluation, governance, facilities, fundraising, and leadership.

2. Prepare a strategic plan to map the future direction of your program. The goals in the program's strategic plan are linked to your priorities for running the program. Think about it for the short term (three to twelve months) and the long term (twelve months to three years). This plan will guide your actions. At the start, ask, "What needs to happen?" And at each evaluation point, ask, "Has it happened?" It is good practice to review the plan monthly, quarterly, semiannually, and annually. If you find yourself switching priorities, it may be that you must reassess and modify the goals.

3. Call for concrete actions in the strategic plan. For example, if one goal is to increase enrollment, you need to consider several actions, such as projecting how many new families you could reasonably enroll, advertising in the community, and offering incentives to families for referrals. The plan helps you maintain your focus. You can then evaluate your progress. If enrollment increases to your satisfaction, the goal is met. Congratulate yourself! If enrollment does not increase, you must decide on another course of action and carry it out.

4. Involve others in your planning and evaluation of the program. If you have an administrative team, do planning and evaluating work together. If you are the only director, plan to involve some members of your staff, compensating them for their time.

5. Ensure that your budget matches the program goals. Money is a measure of the values held by you and your organization, even when funds are scarce. Having a budget helps you be clear in allocating money to your priorities. Reallocation can include finding ways to redistribute internal funds, or it can mean looking for external funds such as grants or loans to supplement the current revenue.

6. Monitor the budget on a continuous process, at least quarterly, though it may be preferable to do a monthly review to reconcile income and expenses. Frequent review helps ensure you are maintaining a financial safety net. Like your personal finances, the fiscal health of your center depends on ongoing check-ins. That practice prevents many problems and saves energy. If you feel uncertain of your skills in this crucial area of administration, consider connecting with First Children's Finance (www.firstchildrensfinance.org) for practical advice and useful tools.

7. Maintain accurate records on finances, enrollment, and personnel allocation and cost. There are many affordable child care management solutions systems that produce great benefits and peace of mind.

8. Have a human resources plan that includes human resource development, personnel expenses, and staff qualification. The *Program Administration Scale (PAS)* (Talan and Bloom 2011) presents a detailed checklist of all the items to consider: orientation, supervision and performance appraisal, staff development, compensation, benefits, and staffing patterns and schedules. For specific information on staff qualifications in your local area, consider the guidance of the Department of Human Services or Department of Education in your state.

9. Foster a positive workplace so staff members are happy to come every day and remain productive. Worker satisfaction is the most important element in staff retention. When people are treated fairly and respectfully, they are more creative and more loyal, and they stay in their jobs longer.

10. Invest in technology to keep the center running smoothly. Have the necessary computers, printers, and internet access for administrative and instructional purposes, and keep all technology well maintained. Include a technology usage plan that protects the privacy of staff, children, and families.

Reflection and Planning

As you finish reading this chapter, reflect on your skills and practices in program administration.

1. Which ideas are familiar, and which are you already using in your daily work?

2. Which ideas would you like to explore further?

3. Choose one or two ideas that you would like to focus on, and use the SMART goal-setting formula to write down your goal:

Specific (What is the specific idea? Who will do it?)	
Measurable (How will you measure success?)	
Achievable (Is it possible to accomplish with the resources you have?)	
Relevant (Will it benefit your particular situation?)	
Time-bound (By when will it happen?)	

CHAPTER 3
MANAGING TIME

Jon had a poster in his office that claimed, "The bad news is time flies. The good news is you're the pilot." That sense of control seemed like a wise perspective to keep in mind, and Jon held on to that viewpoint with intention. He had once felt that he never had enough time. Then he realized the problem was not a shortage of time but how he used the time he had. He decided to plan his time based on his goals rather than on his activities. He made a schedule to fit his goals in program administration, staff support, children's learning, and personal wellness. When he was a teacher, his schedule looked like this: arrival, breakfast, circle time, active learning, large-muscle or outdoor time, story, lunch, nap, active learning, snack, large-muscle or outdoor time, departure. As a director, his schedule looks like this: arrival and greetings of staff and families; administrative closed-door office time; visits to classrooms; lunch; meditation time; planned meetings with individual teachers during naptime; visits to classrooms; goodbyes to families, children, and staff at departure. Jon alternates his morning arrival and afternoon schedules during the week to be able to see all staff every week, both openers and closers.

Parallels between Teaching and Leading

Skilled teachers understand the importance of schedules in running a smooth classroom. A defined sequence within a general time frame helps the children know what to expect. Snack is before outdoor play, then story time comes right after. The sequence of activities is more critical than the exact time of each activity. A daily routine allows for a predictable rhythm that, on the best days, just hums along. The agenda is not rigid; it can be modified if an unexpected situation arises, such as rain or a particularly exciting discovery of bugs in the playground. For education leaders, the same principles apply. A regular daily routine allows directors to balance their time between office work, classroom observations, formal meetings, and informal interactions.

Important Considerations

Time can be a big challenge for anyone—unless we learn to tame it. If we don't manage our time, we will feel like it is managing us. We fret and wonder where time has gone. When that happens, it's a good idea to keep a log of activities for a few days. Then it's possible to identify what tasks took this time and determine whether they were the best use of precious minutes or hours.

Time and goals must be aligned through actions that are relevant. For example, if a leader's goal is to develop professional relationships with their staff, they must take the time to connect with each staff member in formal and informal ways, using multiple modes such as in person, by text, and with handwritten notes. In *Evaluating and Supporting Early Childhood Teachers*, I calculated that it takes about 237 hours per year to create and manage a solid evaluation and support system. This is about 12 percent of a leader's time that yields a great benefit. Likewise, leaders must consider the time needs of other goals, such as implementing a new curriculum or opening an extra classroom. As the leader takes actions that correspond to the goal, it translates into real hours and days of the schedule. It's also the case for all the other tasks on a leader's list, such as visiting classrooms on a regular basis or inspecting the safety of the playground equipment. These tasks will not happen in a timely fashion unless they are marked specifically on your calendar.

Practical Applications

Apply a Diversity and Equity Lens to Managing Time

Time can be described as a contemporary Western cultural construct, and for some it brings annoying constraints when compared to the more laid-back pace of other cultures. The reality is more complex. An early childhood center serves adult family members who have jobs that are bound by the clock, be it in a hospital or a grocery store, so the hours of operation are nonnegotiable. However, leaders can provide flexibility in scheduling that includes sensitivity for the diverse needs of staff members. For example, they design a fair and transparent system where a set number of hours per month is pooled and reserved for employees to meet personal needs for flex time. If the issue of time becomes a source of cultural tension, plan a formal conversation with your staff, using the NAEYC *Code of Ethical Conduct* and the skilled dialogue method (Barrera and Kramer 2017).

In this short video, Dr. Barrera explains the principles of skilled dialogue as finding a solution that considers what's best for children, families, and staff. (*Introducing the Skilled Dialogue Approach*—Brookes Publishing Co.)

Strategies for Managing Time

1. Design your day and week as a teacher would do. It might include arrival, greetings, paperwork, planning, classroom observation, group meetings, individual meetings, wellness (more on this in chapter 12), and departure. Review your week on Friday so that when you return on Monday, the plan is pretty much set, allowing for some flexibility.

2. Have written policies about time for the whole program, with cleaning schedules, playground use, staff breaks, and so on. Think about what is flexible and what is nonnegotiable.

3. Be vigilant on how you use your own time. If you start feeling overwhelmed, keep a log of your activities for a week. Make it simple by jotting your notes in a small notebook you carry with you. Then analyze your results.

4. Be intentional about creating planning time. It is necessary for leaders to run the center well. Ideally a leader should spend about 30 percent of their time on planning in order to make good decisions. Think about scheduling two to three hours a day for planning time, either alone or with a team, be it about the budget, the staffing schedule, or family meetings. Just as teachers cannot be expected to jump into the classroom without having thought out their actions in advance, directors should not jump into the program's operations without advance planning.

5. Control your open-door policy with a method that is clear and friendly, letting families and staff know the pattern, such as posting a note on your door: "I am doing planning work until 2:30 p.m. Then I will be available to talk." Directors who keep the door open all the time find it challenging to deal with constant interruptions. They end up frustrated and not attentive to their visitors, which is unfriendly. Decide on set times when your door is open and when it is closed. This allows you to concentrate on your administrative tasks. Then when you reopen the door, you are more responsive.

6. Alternate your daily schedule during the week to be present at opening and closing times to be available to all staff and families; some days you are on-site early in the morning and leave earlier in the afternoon, and vice versa. This day bookending routine allows you to expand your connections with workers and family members without overtaxing your time.

7. Make screen time as efficient as possible. The average adult spends about eight hours on screens per day, with two and a half hours on social media. Decide the essential function of screens to do your job and control your time by setting your electronic devices to record usage.

8. Manage procrastination. It may be more appealing to spend an hour in the infant room than to finish the grant proposal. But there is a cost when you find yourself writing late into the night. If you notice procrastination has become an annoying habit, turn the time around: write the grant first and then reward yourself with an hour with the babies.

9. Ask your staff or colleagues to share with you any ways they think you might be wasting your time. Consider ways to delegate some tasks that can be done by others.

10. Give yourself permission to follow the proverb that says, "Besides the noble wisdom to getting things done, there is the noble art of leaving things undone." You can find out any nonessentials by looking at your activities log. Then you can let go of them without guilt.

Reflection and Planning

As you finish reading this chapter, reflect on your own use of time.

1. Which ideas are familiar, and which are you already using in your daily work?

2. Which ideas would you like to explore further?

3. Choose one or two ideas that you would like to focus on, and use the SMART goal-setting formula to write down your goal:

Specific (What is the specific idea? Who will do it?)	
Measurable (How will you measure success?)	
Achievable (Is it possible to accomplish with the resources you have?)	
Relevant (Will it benefit your particular situation?)	
Time-bound (By when will it happen?)	

CHAPTER 4
CREATING A CARING
COMMUNITY OF WORKERS

Sara had been a teacher in a program where the climate was negative. Gossip was rampant. Staff did not share materials. Sarcasm was more frequent than affirmations. Problems were not resolved. And children's behavior was a constant concern. It was a stressful environment not representative of the NAEYC principles of quality education. That negative experience motivated Sara to do things differently when she became a director. As a teacher is expected to create a caring community of learners, she creates a caring community of workers. Her strategies are focused. She greets staff with a smile every day; she shows enthusiasm for the work they do together; she anticipates problems, and she helps to resolve them when they occur; she listens; she provides comfort for professional and personal issues. Along the way, Sara expects the same behavior of her staff with one another, and she coaches to that effect. The rewards are tangible: the climate in her center is positive for everyone, adults and children.

Parallels between Teaching and Leading

Children thrive in our early childhood environments when they know they have a place. Teachers show them that their actions and feelings matter. They see educators adjust their behavior to help them grow and learn. Sometimes it is through smiles and enthusiastic encouragement. Other times it is through setting limits and teaching appropriate behavior. Whether the moment is happy or serious, children feel they are important and worthy of care and respect. When directors treat educators as they want them to treat the children, with care, direction, and fairness, they demonstrate that they value them. Pragmatically, this parallel process has the benefit of increasing retention.

Important Considerations

Leading an early childhood program is knowledge work and relationship-based work, just like teaching. An early childhood program is a place where children, families, and staff interact intimately. Emotions can run high. To be available to children, educators need to replenish their own supply of emotional strength. Smiling directors create a caring environment in many ways. They greet staff members every morning, ask how they are, and listen. They model enthusiasm for the work of educating children.

As leaders go about meeting the overall goals of education and care, they work on the goals of administration and finance. This management function is important in maintaining a stable organization that delivers physical safety, adequate staffing, working equipment, staff support and evaluation, and timely paychecks. Workers' sense of well-being depends on this stability. They are relieved from worrying about logistics when they see the leader attending to center operations. It frees them to do the direct job of caring for and educating children, and they are more relaxed in their interactions with one another. They can better celebrate and recognize the result of their joint efforts: the children's learning, the appreciation of families, and their professional relationships.

Leaders put themselves in the minds of their staff members. Prevention is the best strategy for behavior guidance of children. It means anticipating potential problems that can derail order, such as abrupt transitions, a new food, or even a sudden rain shower that keeps everyone indoors. Successful leaders anticipate their staff needs in this same way. They ask themselves, "What is the worker feeling? What do they need to do their job better? What do I need to do to facilitate meeting their needs?"

Practical Applications

Apply a Diversity and Equity Lens to Creating a Caring Community of Workers

Early education is an entry to the workplace for many immigrants and new workers. As stated in the NAEYC position statement on equity, leaders must recognize the value of employing a diverse group of staff. They create a caring community of workers who feel mutually valued when there are opportunities to know one another's personalities, interests, and abilities in an atmosphere that is respectful of differences. For that, leaders must be aware, alert, and intentional about embracing diversity, including their own, on a daily basis. Leaders communicate clearly the ethical principle that the center is a safe place to work and learn. In a well-functioning diverse work environment, the leader sets the tone so everyone feels comfortable and open when having serious discussions surrounding values and bias, as well as in lighthearted banter about music preferences. The leader can offer formal professional development workshops on learning styles or facilitate the exchange of cultural perspectives on the care and education of children. They can also create informal opportunities by offering staff the option to share their favorite desserts at monthly staff meetings.

Strategies for Creating a Caring Community of Workers

1. Treat new staff with care. Ask new hires questions about what they feel they are particularly good at and what they want to contribute to your center. Pay attention to their interests and needs as well as your own so you can match them. If the person has good qualities but not all the background knowledge or skills you would hope for, immediately commit to coaching and supporting them.

2. Design an onboarding process that welcomes each worker professionally. Whatever their job title, new employees look for a job with potential for growth, a positive organizational climate, helpful leadership, clear direction, and work-life balance. Make these conditions clear in your interview, your employee manual, and your welcome packet and introduction to the rest of the team.

3. Pay fairly. Educators know the field has limitations in funding, yet some centers manage to provide better pay and benefits than others, working with similar demographics and conditions. Research the market in your area and design the best compensation package within your budget. The salary scale, benefits, and personnel policies must be transparent so all staff feel that they work in an equitable environment.

4. Create cooperative working conditions that support inexperience and reward experience. This follows the spirit of fairness in the point above. You may pair educators to work together on projects for the center according to their interests, like sharing art ideas, choosing books for a particular theme, and so on. As a teacher would when organizing groups of children, consider natural affinities and complementary personalities.

5. Affirm workers' efforts daily. A positive comment, such as "Emma, good to see you today! I notice you are reading *Corduroy* at circle time—fun book. Let me know how it goes," will make Emma's step a little lighter as she prepares for her preschoolers. Her director has shown interest in her work by reading her lesson plan and commenting on it.

6. Encourage a culture of collaboration. Ensure that educators in different classrooms have many opportunities to exchange materials or ideas for curriculum. Watch for rivalries or hoarding mentalities to divert them as they develop, for example by setting processes to facilitate sharing. In one program, the director organizes a

meeting every quarter to swap toys and materials. It is a positive, lively event that promotes camaraderie and generates creative educational solutions.

7. Do not allow gossip. In early education, we deal daily with intimate details of children's, and families' lives. We like people's stories. This makes it easy to be lax about confidentiality. Gossip is an occupational hazard of caring professions that must be addressed directly to avoid negative consequences on the climate of the center. Use the NAEYC *Code of Ethical Conduct* (NAEYC 2011) as your guide. Explain that gossip does not just hurt staff but harms the education of children as they feel tension among the adults. Repeat the message as often as necessary. Provide training if you feel an outside authority would be more convincing.

8. Be intentional in developing teams, not cliques. Cliques emerge on their own when leadership does not facilitate healthy habits of communication. Like a winning sports team, work teams are created by the organization and nurtured through common goals and activities.

9. Promote mutual regard for all the positions in the center. Everyone has a critical function, whether they work in the kitchen, the classroom, or the office. All these roles complement one another to provide the best care and education to children and service to families. As you repeat this message with examples, workers learn to appreciate one another's value in their common mission. Thank the custodian for maintaining a space that is clean and welcoming for everyone, thank the office clerk for getting payroll done on time every month, thank the teachers for finding creative ways to teach early math, and so on.

10. Bring playfulness to work. Some centers find playful ways to connect, such as designating a funny shoes or hat day. Others share sweet cartoons about teaching young children. Rather than being the organizer yourself, engage a small group of staff members to plan. Set simple ground rules of goodwill. These activities work well when the spirit is positive and there is no pressure to participate.

Reflection and Planning

As you finish reading this chapter, reflect on your practices for creating a caring community of workers.

1. Which ideas are familiar, and which are you already using in your daily work?

2. Which ideas would you like to explore further?

3. Choose one or two ideas that you would like to focus on, and use the SMART goal-setting formula to write down your goal:

Specific (What is the specific idea? Who will do it?)	
Measurable (How will you measure success?)	
Achievable (Is it possible to accomplish with the resources you have?)	
Relevant (Will it benefit your particular situation?)	
Time-bound (By when will it happen?)	

CHAPTER 5
SUPPORTING STAFF'S SKILLS

Teacher Paul has a good rapport with children, but in his room there are many behavior problems, and the space is also cluttered. Director Gabriel has asked Paul to organize the environment better, but Paul says it's just his style. Gabriel is concerned. Paul's work style is unacceptable, and he believes it is time to act. First, Gabriel conducts three short observations in one week. For each one, he videotapes children's actions in the room during circle time and during active learning. Each segment is one to three minutes long. At circle time, children sit tightly in a small space, surrounded by storage boxes of materials. There is no wiggle room and children elbow each other, distracted from the story. During active learning, the shelves are overcrowded with toys, making it difficult for children to find what interests them. They roam around the room not able to choose what they want to do. They chase each other and end up in trouble. Gabriel invites Paul to a meeting at the end of the day in the classroom so they can look at the layout. He talks to Paul about the positives, such as the good rapport he has with the children. Then he brings up his concern about the children's behaviors, and they watch the videos together. They analyze the reasons for the conflicts or lack of engagement and agree that the space is not adequate. They tour the classroom, seeing it through the children's eyes. They decide how to make more room for the circle. They discuss how to make the toys more relevant by thinning the shelves and putting some in storage. With the changes to the environment, the children's play and behavior improve quickly. Paul's professional competence and self-esteem improve too.

> **Parallels between Teaching and Leading**
>
> Intentional teachers assess children's skills and design their instruction accordingly. They propose activities that are safe and help children grow, scaffolding their learning. For a toddler teacher, this might look like helping the little ones practice fine-motor skills with big crayons. The education leader must be intentional too. Leaders can use the same techniques as a toddler teacher to support the professional growth of teachers and other staff. They can be as thoughtful in the process of scaffolding skills as director Gabriel is with teacher Paul in the story. Gabriel does not just let Paul figure out what to do on his own. He takes time and is intentional in helping Paul analyze the situation and involving him in making needed and positive changes.

Important Considerations

The director is the pedagogical leader of the program. Leaders in any field are more effective and respected when they demonstrate caring management skills combined with technical credibility. In early education, it means that they are skilled at teaching children and well informed. They don't just say, "When I was a teacher, I did it this way . . ." Their message is that they are knowledgeable about early childhood education because they continue to learn current research and best practices.

Teaching is a complex set of skills, and not all educators are at the same level. We can consider a teacher's skill through three aspects of teaching quality:

- acts of teaching—what the teacher does directly with the children in the classroom

- results of teaching—what children learn as a result of the acts of teaching

- professional behaviors—behaviors that make a teacher a good worker

Early educators tend to have a low sense of efficacy. When an observer makes positive comments about their classroom, they often respond, "Oh! They are such good children!" They generally do not take credit for their good work, and in the busyness of their days, they cannot tell how well they are doing. The education leader has the important job of being the mirror that affirms an educator's value. On the other hand, if the leader notices that some things are not going well, they must give feedback too. This feedback must be coupled with individual support, such as coaching and professional development.

Practical Applications

Apply a Diversity and Equity Lens to Supporting Staff Skills

The leader must be intentional in recruiting, developing, and retaining a diverse work team and must recognize that not all staff start with the necessary background or develop at the same rate. As with children, the skills of each staff member must be considered individually first. After reviewing the different needs, the leader decides what menu of training and coaching to offer to the whole group and to individuals. That often means budgeting additional time and money, but it is an investment in your staff to increase their skill and professional confidence. For example, you may hire immigrant staff for their cultural sensitivity and the ability to speak a language other than English. But they may not have the early education or bilingual skills necessary for quality work. Accordingly, you must increase the professional development allocation to include technical training in ECE and English classes so these valuable workers can attain the level of expertise needed to teach all children well.

Strategies for Supporting Staff Skills

1. Make a plan to evaluate and support your staff. If there is no system in place, I recommend you use a guide such as my book *Evaluating and Supporting Early Childhood Teachers* (Passe 2015) or take a class in your area or online to help you set up a system that will work for you and your center. The first goal is to recognize good performance. The second goal is to support staff with performance problems so they improve.

2. Evaluate staff members in the three aspects of their job (acts of teaching, results of teaching, and professional behaviors). These concepts also apply to any job in your organization, including building maintenance, accounting, or food preparation.

3. Assess classroom quality with credible tools, such as the Early Childhood Environment Rating Scales (ECERS), the Early Language and Literacy Classroom Observation (ELLCO), or the Classroom Assessment Scoring System (CLASS). These validated instruments guide the observer to be objective through the use of solid checklists with a rubric.

4. Involve staff in their own evaluation. Whether you use observation forms from the instruments mentioned above or your own tools, the process should not be one-way. Ask staff to self-assess before you discuss their performance together. The objective is to have a professional conversation that identifies strengths and clarifies areas for improvement. This is a motivating approach that engages staff in their performance.

5. Write a performance review summary with a growth plan and SMART goals (Specific, Measurable, Achievable, Relevant, and Time-bound). Follow up with the actions you have agreed on. It is not fair to let employees figure out things on their own. They deserve the director's respectful and steady support to grow in their profession.

6. Give periodic feedback when things are going well: "Jon, I noticed how you helped Mason and his mom separate this morning. She looked reassured when she left." "Margo, good idea to take the literacy bucket outside! I saw how the children were so engaged in writing and scribbling." Keep a small notebook in your back pocket where you can jot down specific affirmations. These affirmations can be given verbally or in a text or email.

7. Give feedback when things are not going well. This is a more formal situation that can only be handled in person, not by a text or email. If the situation is a safety emergency, handle it immediately. If it is a concern about a teaching action, set a meeting with the teacher to discuss it in private: "Kim, I noticed how you sent Lani to the time-out chair today during circle time. It seems to be a recurring problem. I want to take some time to process with you what happened and how we can make it easier for you and Lani. Please meet me in my office during naptime; Eva will cover for you."

8. Provide professional development to the group and to individuals. Some trainings are mandatory and required by licensing rules, such as first aid and mandated reporting. Other trainings should be aligned with your goals for the program, such as early literacy or behavior guidance. Other offerings should be specific to growth goals for each staff member.

9. Provide opportunities for professional sharing after training events to solidify learning. For example, you may put up a poster in the staff lounge with the title "What I Learned at the Behavior Guidance Workshop." Expect staff members to write their thoughts. A natural outcome of this strategy is that you will see more exchanges happen informally.

10. Organize a mentoring system to pair experienced educators with educators who are new to the profession. This is a good way to generate positive feelings of collegiality in the team. The mentees learn additional skills and grow in confidence. The mentors appreciate the professional recognition and the opportunity to contribute their wisdom and knowledge.

Reflection and Planning

As you finish reading this chapter, reflect on your practices in supporting staff skills.

1. Which ideas are familiar, and which are you already using in your daily work?

2. Which ideas would you like to explore further?

3. Choose one or two ideas that you would like to focus on, and use the SMART goal-setting formula to write down your goal:

Specific (What is the specific idea? Who will do it?)	
Measurable (How will you measure success?)	
Achievable (Is it possible to accomplish with the resources you have?)	
Relevant (Will it benefit your particular situation?)	
Time-bound (By when will it happen?)	

CHAPTER 6
PROMOTING
CHILDREN'S LEARNING

Molly is the new director at Little Explorers Preschool. The departing director warned her about persistent behavior problems in Room B. In this classroom, the children are often in conflict. Several have taken on the habit of escaping into the hallways, even after special doorknobs were installed. Three teachers have quit in six months. Molly decides to observe and assess the situation. In her first week, she visits the classroom every day at different times of the day. She takes notice of the children first: wandering from center to center, not attending to the story, and fighting over toys. Four little boys have been labeled troublemakers. She notices the teachers trying to manage inappropriate behavior with alternating threats and pleas. She asks for lesson plans and children's assessments, but there are none. She sees that some activities are set out, but there is no coherent curriculum to grab the children's attention and engage them productively. If an organized curriculum had ever been in use, the teachers are no longer following it. Given that these children are going to kindergarten next year, Molly recognizes that their learning will be compromised unless the teachers implement a more robust curriculum and assessment strategy, so she researches and orders a new curriculum. She trains the teachers to use it, and she coaches them to ensure fidelity. She likewise invests in an assessment tool. With this plan, the results are positive: within a few weeks, there are fewer behavior problems and more learning opportunities for the children. The teachers feel supported in their skills and are more confident and satisfied.

> **Parallels between Teaching and Leading**
>
> Teachers have the direct responsibility to ensure that all children in their group learn the skills that are appropriate for their age and development, whether that means supporting toddlers as they go down the slide or helping preschoolers learn to count to ten. Education leaders are also responsible for children's learning, but at one remove. They are the instructional leaders, responsible for the big picture of teaching and learning. They not only ask, "What are the children learning?" and "How do we know they are learning?" but their primary question must be "What do the teachers need to ensure that teaching happens and the children learn?" In the parallel process mindset, education leaders use the same skills as teachers: they assess the skills of educators and support them so they continue to learn and grow.

Important Considerations

When children are not learning, some educators have a tendency to find fault with the children or families, citing problems associated with family lifestyle, poverty, disorganization, trauma, or the children's physical or mental health. That thinking is risky. It blocks one's ability to find ethical educational solutions.

In fact, the ethics of our profession tell us that it is more important to look at barriers to learning that are external to the child and family. These may be related to problems with teacher skills, or they can stem from an environment that is not developmentally appropriate, inadequate curriculum, or ineffective leadership in supporting the competence of staff and good organization of a center. In the case of Little Explorers Preschool, it was all four before Molly arrived. Molly assessed the situation correctly and found solutions.

Educational leaders must hold on to the conviction that all children in their center or program can learn to their highest individual potential. They act on that conviction by supporting early educators. They do so with evaluation, finding educators' strengths and weaknesses, coaching to improve teaching skills, and providing resources such as professional development or educational materials.

Practical Applications

Apply a Diversity and Equity Lens to Promoting Children's Learning

Demonstrate commitment to equitable outcomes by arranging actions and budgets so you provide the training, coaching, staffing, materials, assessments, and planning time to fulfill the mission of your program that "all children will learn." Use children's assessments as strong evidence in the "results of teaching" aspect of teacher quality. If students are not making progress, it's important to analyze all the possible factors for the failure to learn, rather than assuming the children are the barriers to their own learning. Then be intentional in finding solutions in all areas of the program to ensure that the environment is culturally appropriate, fitting the children's and families' learning styles and interests. Provide these students, individually or as a group, with varied instructional approaches, such as a curriculum with more hands-on learning activities, more explicit instruction, or new topics of discovery to catch their attention.

Strategies for Promoting Children's Learning

1. Follow the principles of NAEYC's *Developmentally Appropriate Practice*, the NAEYC *Code of Ethical Conduct*, and NAEYC's *Advancing Equity in Early Childhood Education* position statement. Two recommendations are especially relevant here: "5. Involve children, families, and the community in the design and implementation of learning activities"; and "6. Actively promote children's agency" (NAEYC 2019).

2. Set the expectation that all children will learn, not just in words but also through actions that show your commitment. If teachers become discouraged, you are the leader in this movement who keeps the idea alive by providing resources and encouragement while identifying successes. You may need to have intensive conversations with some educators.

3. Use best practices in early education: planning curriculum, teaching the children, assessing the children, and evaluating the entire process in a continuous loop.

4. Keep up with research and innovation in early education. Be intentional about allocating time for reading and discussing research with other directors and your staff. Technical knowledge enhances your credibility as an educator.

5. Attend the same professional development workshops as your staff. It is common to hear early educators in professional development workshops say, "I wish my director was here to hear this," usually in response to information that is contradicted by leadership directives at the center. For example, perhaps the center has a rule that children's drawings should be displayed on bulletin boards that are four feet high.

This height is too high according to best practice, which calls for displaying children's work at eye level to promote pride in their work.

6. Observe classrooms with a holistic lens. Leaders are often called into classrooms to observe a child's challenging behavior(s), but there is deep risk in that kind of narrow focus when the solution becomes making the child comply. A comprehensive approach looks at the context for the child, such as curriculum activities, transitions, teacher affect and language, and physical space. This bigger picture is a better model for discovering how to help the child learn and modifying instruction for best outcomes, rather than trying to "fix" the child.

7. Invest in tools that assess children's learning with the NAEYC recommendations on equity and developmentally appropriate practice in mind. Ensure that assessments are designed and validated for use with the children being assessed. They should identify children's strengths and provide a well-rounded picture of development.

8. Coach and support your team in using children's assessment data. Review results with your teachers. Teachers know the children's backgrounds and personalities well, so they risk interpreting assessment data subjectively. Education leaders are removed from daily interactions with children. This allows them to look at the data more neutrally. Their objective perspective is useful to generate better educational plans.

9. Use the data to inform instruction and resources. In one classroom, you may find that children are not progressing in literacy. You know from your observations that the teacher does not teach vocabulary in her daily read-aloud. Putting the two together, you and the teacher can discuss how to address the children's learning by teaching vocabulary every day.

10. Celebrate children's learning and the teacher's role in the process. Early childhood education is an isolating job, with the teacher's full day spent tending to all the physical, emotional, and cognitive needs of little people. You can be the mirror that shows teachers how their good work promotes children's learning. You tell teachers that they did it! In that way, you are a cheerleader, instilling the conviction that all children learn because all teachers teach.

Reflection and Planning

As you finish reading this chapter, reflect on your practices in promoting children's learning.

1. Which ideas are familiar, and which are you already using in your daily work?

2. Which ideas would you like to explore further?

3. Choose one or two ideas that you would like to focus on, and use the SMART goal-setting formula to write down your goal:

Specific (What is the specific idea? Who will do it?)	
Measurable (How will you measure success?)	
Achievable (Is it possible to accomplish with the resources you have?)	
Relevant (Will it benefit your particular situation?)	
Time-bound (By when will it happen?)	

CHAPTER 7
COMMUNICATING WELL

Director Eva is the hub of the communication network in her center. She knows everyone and everything that happens. She sees everything, and all come to her with problems and solutions—but this often results in overload, and by the end of the day it is exhausting. Finally, she devises a system to manage this haphazard flow of communication. Her plan includes several modes of communication: personal and group; in person and online; formal and informal. All the modes are aligned. This worked well when she decided to get a new developmental assessment tool. She knew it would raise questions and even create some anxiety, so she communicated in multiple ways. First, she engaged her staff in choosing between two options in person. She followed up with written information. Then she provided training in person. With the families, she began by giving information in the newsletter, and she invited parents to an in-person meeting to learn more. She had a similar process with the advisory board. Along the way, this differentiated approach was effective in getting everyone on the same page. Most important, she gained the trust of all the stakeholders. They saw that she was making an educational decision that would benefit the children, the families, and the staff.

> **Parallels between Teaching and Leading**
>
> In a well-run classroom, we see teachers giving clear directions to children even for routine activities: "Okay, children, after circle time we will go outside, like we do every day. First, go to your cubby and find your coat and hat. Ms. Maria and I will assist you." They use a variety of methods of communicating, such as singing or counting, and they assist some children individually. They assure the children that they are there to help so everyone is successful. Education leaders can use similar techniques to communicate with their staff. They do so by alternating ways of communicating, such as in person (large group, small group, and individually) and also by text or email. Not everyone will understand just because the leader says it once. Whether directors are presenting an assessment tool or explaining new licensing rules about toothbrushing, everyone hears the message more clearly when it is tailored and repeated.

Important Considerations

You are modeling professional communication for your entire staff. Communication is important internally, to avoid confusion among staff and families. It is also critical externally to generate goodwill and positive interest in the community. The message is that "We know what we are doing, and we work and learn together."

Good verbal communication starts with listening. Leaders who listen carefully give full attention to the speaker. They are careful not to betray irritation or disinterest with their body language. "People problems" are often communication problems, verbal or written. Misunderstandings happen over seemingly simple things like tone of voice, gestures, or choice of words. Anything a parent or a staff member says has importance, even if you don't agree with it.

Here are some tips for active listening:

- Ask clarifying questions. Try asking, "What does it feel like?" or "Can you say more?" or repeat their comment and say, "Is that what you mean?"

- Concentrate. People talk at about 150 words per minute but think at about 500 words per minute. So stay focused.

- Listen for key words the speaker repeats that are important for understanding their point of view.

Good written communication is oriented toward the readers. It tells them what they need to know with simple words and short sentences, in plain language and without jargon. The tone is conversational. It is tactful and courteous. This applies to all documents from the program: information brochures, monthly newsletters, memos to staff, and the center's website. Not only does it make the information accessible to all in English, but it also is easier to translate into other languages as needed.

Practical Applications

Apply a Diversity and Equity Lens to Communicating Well

Communication styles are personal and cultural. Many factors influence how people express what they think, want, feel, and need. These factors may include age, education, ethnic background, language, and temperament. Leaders have their own preferred way of communicating too. But to be most effective and minimize misunderstandings to keep things running smoothly, they must pay attention to the diverse recipients of the message. For example, this could mean texting younger workers but giving a written note to older ones. A verbal explanation may be necessary for staff members who are second-language learners. For all, it means using plain language, a direct voice, and a friendly tone.

Strategies for Communicating Well

1. Hold regular face-to-face meetings. A good ratio is to hold large-group meetings once a month, with small-group or classroom meetings every other week. The direct contact builds relationships and promotes a culture of dialogue and problem solving.

2. Use several modes of communication, formal and informal. For formal information, such as announcing an important directive from the health department, announce it in a large-group meeting, verbally and in writing. Then, to reinforce the message, you may follow up informally in small groups and individually. Both formal and informal communication must be aligned, without contradictions.

3. Make expectations clear. In presenting a new assessment tool, unclear communication sounds like this: "Here is the new assessment tool. It will be very useful to see how children grow and to share results with parents at conferences. I hope you like it." On the other hand, clear expectations sound like this: "Here is the new assessment tool. It will be very useful to see how children grow and to share results with parents at conferences. We have three months to practice and get used to it. Take the time to read it, and we will talk about it at our next meeting in two weeks. Then we will make a plan for implementing it." With the second example, recipients of the

message get the information in a direct way and are assured of the leader's support. This increases the chance for success.

4. Use plain language in your communications about program policies, child development, and early childhood education. Educational jargon is difficult for noneducators to understand. Instead of "Family conferences regarding your children's growth and development according to the ECIPS will be held on June 10," say, "On June 10, teachers will meet with parents to talk about what their child is learning."

5. Be wise with electronic communication and social media. They are a good communication tool for positive comments, such as texting an affirmation: "Lucas, thanks for sharing your dramatic play props with the Blue Jays classroom. Nice collaboration with your colleagues!" But they are a volatile instrument for communicating concerns or serious topics that need context and time for reflection.

6. Have a social media and communication policy for all. Leaders must watch for the emotional safety of everyone. Therefore, policies about confidentiality and the use of social media must be included in both the parent handbook and the staff handbook, with ongoing reminders of the importance of not posting unauthorized pictures or stories of children or families, and clearly separating personal accounts from the program's private account.

7. Practice *Watch*, *Wait*, *Listen*, *Respond*. This communication technique gives you time to assess the situation, especially if the other person is upset. It leads to better problem solving and outcomes.

   - *Watch*: note the body language and expression of the speaker; is it relaxed or tense?

   - *Wait*: do not make quick assumptions or offer quick solutions.

   - *Listen*: lean in and concentrate on the speaker's words.

   - *Respond*: keep your tone neutral yet empathetic ("I hear you") or ask a question for clarification ("Tell me more about . . ."). Give yourself time to think more clearly ("Thank you for telling me. I don't have a solution right now. Let me think about it until tomorrow," or "This is a big issue; we need more time. How about we set a meeting for tomorrow to discuss this further and come up with a solution together?").

8. Welcome feedback. Invite staff members to share their thoughts in person or in writing. Some will be tactful and others less so. That's okay. Listen well. You want to learn from the comments.

9. Be alert to circulating rumors. Without good communication from the leader, the rumor mill can develop as an informal system of misinformation. It can be especially

destructive in multilingual teams where gossip is shared among people of the same language.

10. Create a culture of empathy with positive communication. Be alert to tattling, and manage it directly, just as the teacher does in the classroom. Quietly bring the parties together, using "I messages," brainstorming solutions, and agreeing to resolution. Interpersonal conflict is common in early childhood programs, and the levelheaded intervention of the leader brings welcome relief.

Reflection and Planning

As you finish reading this chapter, reflect on your practices in communicating well.

1. Which ideas are familiar, and which are you already using in your daily work?

2. Which ideas would you like to explore further?

3. Choose one or two ideas that you would like to focus on, and use the SMART goal-setting formula to write down your goal:

Specific (What is the specific idea? Who will do it?)	
Measurable (How will you measure success?)	
Achievable (Is it possible to accomplish with the resources you have?)	
Relevant (Will it benefit your particular situation?)	
Time-bound (By when will it happen?)	

CHAPTER 8
WORKING WITH FAMILIES

When a father arrives to pick up his baby, he's surprised to see she's sucking on a pacifier. He and his wife had communicated to her teacher that they didn't want Maya to use pacifiers. Flustered, he takes the pacifier out of the baby's mouth and leaves without saying a word. At home the parents discuss the situation and get increasingly concerned. Did the staff give the pacifier because she was crying too much and that was the only way to console her? Did the teachers disregard their wishes? Or did they just forget? The next morning both parents are in the director's office with tears in their eyes. Director Jamie welcomes them calmly. She acknowledges their feelings. She promises to research the situation and let them know at pickup time. She talks to the lead teacher in the infant room and finds out that a new assistant teacher had given Maya the pacifier after diapering without thinking. The baby was not distressed. Jamie invites the teacher and the assistant to join the meeting at the end of the day with the parents. They discuss the situation and explain what happened. All agree that this was a mistake. Jamie offers to put in place a policy that all staff will review parents' preferences daily. The parents feel reassured by this solution.

Parallels between Teaching and Leading

Like teachers do with children, directors set the tone for relationship building. They use the technique of Watch, Wait, Listen, Respond. They build trust by problem solving with caring empathy. When children are upset, they count on their teachers to guide them to solutions. Families have the same needs. They are leaving their beloved child in an institution, often with mixed feelings. They count on the education leader to be available for the good days but especially for the not-so-good situations, as in the story. As you build trust, the same techniques work for families as for children.

Important Considerations

When working with families, directors have the pedagogical task of preparing parents for their family engagement role in the future. The early years are parents' first engagement in their child's education, and they are learning how to advocate for their baby. The education leader's responsive listening gives them the confidence to continue speaking up throughout their child's educational career.

Parents need the reassuring message that the center and the family will work together to teach the children well. Handing over the care and education of young children to professionals is scary and intimidating for many parents. They worry about their child's well-being. As new parents, they may feel insecure in their own abilities and unsure about what they want and how to ask for it, like the parents in the vignette. They may express their anxiety in aggressive ways, loudly accusing the staff of not doing their job. When that happens, the leader must listen with empathy to deescalate the tension. The parents' position comes from a place of love, and they only want to protect their child, even if educators don't agree with their point of view. Therefore the most effective response is to speak respectfully, without being condescending or dismissive. Use words that validate their strong feelings ("I see that you're upset") and offer problem solving ("I want to find a solution with you").

Children benefit most when families and child care staff develop reciprocal relationships. That happens when parents receive clear information about the center in written form, confirmed with verbal clarifications on all aspects of operations: schedule, fees, calendar, health requirements, and behavior guidance. Reciprocity improves when you ask parents what goals they have for their child and the child's strengths, likes, and dislikes.

Leaders also have the marketing and public relations job of keeping families happy as customers. This is best accomplished by following the suggestions above. Customers are happy when their expectations are met at the right time with the right intention. In the case of child care, the right time is very narrow, based on the age of the child. Parents of infants, toddlers, and preschoolers need very specific services in a small window of time. The right intention is the developmentally appropriate care and education you provide their most precious little people. Happiness is contagious, and happy workers make customers happy. Leaders should be mindful that their care and support of staff is a big contributor to positive relations with families.

Practical Applications

Apply a Diversity and Equity Lens to Working with Families

Sometimes early educators feel that they know best how to care for children, especially if there are differences in the cultural practices of the family and the program or educator. That creates a rivalry that does not serve children well. Education leaders must be alert to this tendency and set the tone for reciprocal relationships with families. Their job is coaching the teachers to see their unique role as collaborators with families. As teachers support and care for the child in the program, they must work at recognizing their personal biases about families, then follow their professional responsibilities and find common ground. This is accomplished through a skilled dialogue approach (Barrera and Kramer 2017), in which the ideas of educators and those of families complement each other.

Strategies for Working with Families

1. Promote a culture in your center that honors families and recognizes that they want the best for their children. Effective early childhood leaders establish a no-fault attitude toward families. Parents may not have technical skills or information about early childhood education, but they want their children to thrive. Your attitude on this matter is an important guide for your staff.

2. Write a direct and user-friendly parent handbook. You want families to clearly understand the language so they see themselves and their child in the handbook— be it in the rules for drop-off and pickup or in the guidelines regarding illness. Be clear on what is nonnegotiable and what is optional. Write the handbook in plain English, eliminating or explaining jargon. It should be no more difficult to read than a parenting magazine article.

3. Make the intake a welcoming event. Explain the bureaucratic tasks and their purpose. Official paperwork can be reassuring in itself, as long as it is done in an atmosphere that is pleasant and unrushed. This first experience should show families that the way their child will be cared for in the center will be consistent with the way they raise their child at home.

4. Check in with families after two or three weeks. View this time as the second welcome. By then parents will be more settled as they have gotten familiar with the environment and can give you more coherent responses. That is a good time to ask families about their interests and their desires for their child. Invite families to participate in the life of the center at different levels. It may be that all they can manage is bringing their child to the center each day. Others may have the time and

energy to come to read to a group or join your advisory board. Reassure them that all are valid types of family involvement.

5. Communicate clearly. Use various forms of communication: family meetings, informal conversation, bulletin boards, notes on paper or by means of an app, email, texting, phone calls, website. This repetition is necessary to catch the attention of busy parents who are juggling many responsibilities.

6. Offer a menu of family support events. Some programs hold sessions on educational topics such as family literacy or behavior guidance. Others propose social events by age group, such as the opportunity to meet other infant families. Others schedule "parents' night out," caring for the children for a couple of hours one evening as a convenience for families. However, the primary responsibility is for care and education during regular operating hours. Consider activities that are workable for you and your staff. They should not be an extra burden.

7. Schedule twice-yearly parent-teacher conferences for a formal review of children's development and learning, based on the assessment data you are collecting.

8. Set the expectation that teachers will make frequent positive contact with families about their children. You may already have a communication app that allows for sending pictures of children in action. This nice visual approach should not be just about cute moments. It must be balanced with written and verbal comments about the child's learning.

9. Help teachers prepare for difficult situations, such as talking to parents about a child's challenges. Provide professional training on techniques like focused observations and skilled dialogue. Make it a firm rule that concerns cannot be expressed casually at drop-off and pickup. Support the teacher directly by attending sensitive family meetings, including coaching before and debriefing after.

10. Conduct simple anonymous surveys and take advantage of the wisdom of your parent advisory board to continue to improve your services and relationships with families. If you do not have an advisory board, consider creating one. As with all other interactions, make a formal pledge of confidentiality to avoid letting rumors and bad feelings circulate.

Reflection and Planning

As you finish reading this chapter, reflect on your practices in working with families.

1. Which ideas are familiar, and which are you already using in your daily work?

2. Which ideas would you like to explore further?

3. Choose one or two ideas that you would like to focus on, and use the SMART goal-setting formula to write down your goal:

Specific (What is the specific idea? Who will do it?)	
Measurable (How will you measure success?)	
Achievable (Is it possible to accomplish with the resources you have?)	
Relevant (Will it benefit your particular situation?)	
Time-bound (By when will it happen?)	

CHAPTER 9
ORGANIZING
THE PHYSICAL SPACE

The consultant visited this program on a Thursday morning. The center was new, with walls painted in bright red, yellow, and blue. Loud music was piped throughout. Rooms and hallways had many colorful decorations. In the director's office, the sounds of crying children and teachers' exasperated voices could be heard even through the closed door. When the visitor remarked that it seemed like a challenging day, the weary director responded that it was Thursday, and this was normal at the end of the week. She had accepted that Thursdays and Fridays were chaotic because the children and staff were overtired. Her tenure was short. She resigned after six months. The next director was not willing to tolerate this situation. She believed that the physical space can have a positive or a negative impact on children's learning and well-being, as well as on staff. In this case, the environment was harsh and overstimulating. It was a not a good place for teaching and learning. She and the staff redesigned the environment to intentionally facilitate belonging and support engagement. They reexamined the use of background music and eliminated it except for quiet music at the beginning of naptime. They took down decorations that did not have an instructional purpose, replacing them with children's drawings and family pictures. They organized the clutter and repainted the walls in soft colors. The result was a calmer and more productive environment, even at the end of the week.

> **Parallels between Teaching and Leading**
>
> In a well-organized classroom, teachers make the space attractive and usable by children. The furnishings are child sized. The materials and toys are easily accessible and developmentally appropriate. There are areas for large-group, small-group, and individual activities. There is a balance of hard and soft surfaces for exploration and comfort. Teachers consider the space "the third teacher" so children build trust and self-confidence, knowing they belong.
>
> Leaders of early childhood centers have the same goal: to build trust and self-confidence for all who enter the building. They apply the same attention to attractiveness, accessibility, comfort, and safety for everyone—children, families, and staff.

Important Considerations

The physical environment of an early childhood center is worthy of special attention when we consider that children in full-time care may spend up to 12,500 hours of their lives in it by the time they are five years old. Their center truly is "home away from home."

Sounds, colors, and lighting have a significant impact on the behavior of children and adults. They can contribute to a sense of calm when they are muted and controlled. Conversely, they can be overstimulating and distracting so that at the end of the day or the week, everyone is at wit's end, as in the story.

Clutter is a hazard in our culture of abundance. In a cluttered classroom, it is difficult for children to find materials or select toys for meaningful play. Clutter raises sensory stimulation and creates overload, which generates behavior problems and loss of learning. In a cluttered office, documents get lost in piles and efficiency is compromised. It takes more time to organize the work of running a program. In a cluttered storage closet, staff cannot find the materials they need, which leads to overspending as they repurchase items they already have.

Practical Applications

Apply a Diversity and Equity Lens to Organizing the Physical Space

We develop an impression as soon as we enter an early childhood center. It can be positive or negative. It is rarely neutral. Does it feel clean, safe, warm, friendly, and inviting to *all* families, children, and staff? First, the center must follow all the local safety and accessibility codes. With a diversity and equity lens, the setup also should offer amenities for everyone, such as privacy nooks for nursing mothers and for staff to conduct personal business during their break. The toys are placed on the shelves so children have easy access at all times. The furniture is arranged to meet diverse abilities. The sounds are those of educators and children playing, singing, talking, comforting, and laughing. The books, materials, toys, and wall postings reflect the community of the center. All the users of the space feel like they belong and it is *their* place. At the same time, the environment is flexible to welcome and integrate new arrivals and visitors.

Strategies for Organizing the Physical Space

1. Tour your own center and notice how you feel. Take pictures with your phone and look at them the next day. Decide how the space meets your criteria for welcome, safety, and comfort. This exercise might encourage you to keep things as they are or prompt you to make changes.

2. Make hallways friendly, with welcome signs, pictures of staff with their bios, and bulletin boards with children's work. Write signs in various languages if appropriate for your population.

3. Arrange the classrooms to facilitate optimal conditions for playing and learning, according to best practices in early education as documented in environment tools like the ELLCO or the ECERS.

4. Post children's drawings and work in the classrooms at eye level so children can see themselves and one another.

5. Design the outdoor spaces with the same care for the playing, learning, teaching, and comfort of children and adults. Plan for a sensory table as well as dramatic play, art, science, and literacy experiences. Place benches strategically for reading stories and to give adults an occasional place to sit.

6. Arrange the environment to promote good working conditions for staff. Working with young children means often sitting on small chairs and squatting on the floors. For their breaks, adults need to be able to relax in adult-sized furniture in a separate staff lounge and restroom. Providing cubicles that allow for private business during break time is also a mark of respect for workers.

7. Designate a comfortable place (not a bathroom) for mothers, including staff, to breastfeed or pump their milk in privacy, if they desire.

8. Maintain a separate office space for administrators for private conversations and meetings.

9. Declutter and clean all spaces to offer a safe, healthy, and organized appearance that demonstrates hygiene and good order. See the center the way prospective families see it when they take their first tour. They must be able to imagine their child in a wholesome and child-friendly environment.

10. Have a system of routine maintenance for all areas of the program indoors and outdoors. This is critical for safety and comfort, and it is also smart financially because ongoing small repairs are less stressful and expensive than a big project forced by delayed maintenance.

Reflection and Planning

As you finish reading this chapter, reflect on your practices in organizing the physical space.

1. Which ideas are familiar, and which are you already using in your daily work?

2. Which ideas would you like to explore further?

3. Choose one or two ideas that you would like to focus on, and use the SMART goal-setting formula to write down your goal:

Specific (What is the specific idea? Who will do it?)	
Measurable (How will you measure success?)	
Achievable (Is it possible to accomplish with the resources you have?)	
Relevant (Will it benefit your particular situation?)	
Time-bound (By when will it happen?)	

CHAPTER 10
PROVIDING CURRICULUM
AND MATERIALS

The website of Bright Little Scholars Program describes the use of a well-known curriculum. The detailed explanation assures the public that the children are receiving developmentally appropriate care and instruction. When director Alice is hired, she is surprised to be met with blank stares when she asks the staff how they use the curriculum, and she finds dusty manuals on the office shelf. Classroom observations confirm that there is no evidence that this curriculum is being implemented, so Alice tackles curriculum implementation as her first project. She involves the lead teachers in examining it and choosing priorities, such as developing a simple lesson plan to document teaching and learning activities. She organizes an all-staff training to present it and establish general directions for its use. She then follows up with individualized support for staff who need assistance and coaching. The result is improved quality for the center. The most rewarding aspect is that children become more engaged because the activities and the materials are more stimulating. The ultimate success is that children's assessments show improvement in the areas of language and literacy and social development, and the educators' professional satisfaction increases accordingly.

Parallels between Teaching and Leading

Teaching is both science and art. Science comes from the curriculum and its appropriateness to the developmental education of children. Art comes as teachers adapt the curriculum to make it work so all children can learn from it. The same principles apply for the leader responsible for the curriculum. The science for leaders lies in training the staff in its general use, then the art comes in finding multiple ways to individualize support so early educators can implement it with confidence and skill.

Important Considerations

Maintaining a high-quality curriculum is a critical aspect of pedagogical leadership. It is an ongoing process for the education leader and the staff. When possible, involving teachers and even families in choosing a new curriculum is a good strategy.

The reason for the use of a particular curriculum must be clear. It should be aligned to the mission and goals of the program and to quality standards. Curricula may be packaged (a book or set of books with learning activities, usually organized by themes, topics, or projects) or emergent (teachers pull activities from a variety of sources, following children's interests). Either way, it is critical to determine that the curriculum addresses all areas of development according to ECE standards.

A mark of program quality is how the curriculum is evident. A common criterion is that the room should "scream the theme," not just in the materials but also in samples of work that children are doing during their explorations. If children are learning about insects, there should be many examples of the study of insects around the room: paintings, a chart paper with children's comments (dictated to their teacher), an entomology lab in the dramatic play center, children using magnifying glasses on the playground to observe bugs, books about insects in the library, and the reading of *Ladybug at Orchard Avenue* at circle time.

Providing curriculum is just the first part—the follow-up is more important than the acquisition of the curriculum. Leaders are responsible for guiding their staff in implementing the curriculum with fidelity. Otherwise, it can become loosely related activities that entertain the children but do not achieve the goals of scaffolding their growth in all areas of development. Some teachers will be more autonomous than others, based on their level of experience or their affinity for the tool itself.

Practical Applications

Apply a Diversity and Equity Lens to Curriculum and Materials

The curriculum must reflect the children's lives and experiences while also presenting new ideas to expand their learning. That is the NAEYC concept of "mirrors" (who the children, families, and staff are and what they know about a topic) and "windows" (new ideas and skills they are learning and exploring). The mirrors are not meant to be a stereotypical interpretation from the teachers' perspective only. Rather, they must be a reflection of the children's previous knowledge about the topic, as well as their families' ideas. To consider these "mirrors," practice the KWL Model: Know, Want-to-know, and Learned. To continue the previous example about the study of insects, we would see teachers leading a conversation about what preschoolers *know* about insects and about what they *want* to know. Then during several weeks of exploration, the children and adults would talk about what they are *learning*. The "windows" are new information that the teachers add from books and scientific knowledge. Applying this mindset guarantees that the curriculum will meet diversity and equity standards on any topic or area of study. Support your early educators in keeping "mirrors" and "windows" in the forefront as they plan learning activities.

Strategies for Curriculum and Materials

1. Assess the curriculum currently in use in the program and decide whether it is implemented adequately. This will inform you how to proceed—whether everything is going well or you need to do more training or find a new curriculum.

2. Provide general training on using the curriculum to all staff and be clear about the expectations. Set a timeline for full implementation. Assure staff that you have support in place, such as periodic observations to see how it is going and listening sessions to problem solve possible challenges.

3. Pay for planning time and expect that teachers will document how they implement the curriculum with lesson planning and teaching delivery with activities. Put the expectation in the staff handbook.

4. Involve the staff in choosing a consistent lesson plan format for all the classrooms. It may be organized by areas of development or by learning areas. When everyone uses the same form, it is easier for you to glance at the information and give feedback. Explain that the exercise is not merely paperwork. It is a way to ensure that learning activities and materials are prepared in advance.

5. If you do have a curriculum but do not see sufficient evidence of it being used, assess the reason. As you do teacher evaluations, focus on curriculum implementation and have a conversation with the educators. There may be lack of interest, skill, or time management. Keep up the expectation and adjust your coaching to help teachers so they can feel confident and successful.

6. Follow quality standards for materials and equipment such as the Early Childhood Environment Rating Scales or the NAEYC accreditation criteria.

7. Coach educators on making the most of the curriculum through differentiation, adjusting instruction and materials to meet the individual needs of learners.

8. Review and assess the educational needs of children before purchasing new materials and toys. Engage staff to research and propose items that are developmentally appropriate.

9. Have a system for rotating materials to maintain the interest of children. Provide containers, a clean and accessible storage space, and paid staff time to do the rotation.

10. Celebrate the successful implementation of the curriculum. It may be by posting pictures of children's work in the hallways, inviting families to a curriculum party, or sharing classroom projects at staff meetings. It is important to highlight how you are all going in the same direction. In one of the centers I visited that had an early literacy initiative, the kitchen staff contributed to the curriculum by writing the menu on a large whiteboard and reading it aloud to the children every day at lunchtime.

Reflection and Planning

As you finish reading this chapter, reflect on your practices in providing curriculum and materials.

1. Which ideas are familiar, and which are you already using in your daily work?

2. Which ideas would you like to explore further?

3. Choose one or two ideas that you would like to focus on, and use the SMART goal-setting formula to write down your goal:

Specific (What is the specific idea? Who will do it?)	
Measurable (How will you measure success?)	
Achievable (Is it possible to accomplish with the resources you have?)	
Relevant (Will it benefit your particular situation?)	
Time-bound (By when will it happen?)	

CHAPTER 11
DEALING WITH CHALLENGING BEHAVIORS: CHILDREN, STAFF, AND FAMILIES

Director Julie arrived at the center with good energy that morning. As she was hanging her coat on the hook, teacher Ana came into the office yelling, "I can't stand it anymore: my assistant is late again. You need to fix this!" Later that morning, Julie got a text from an angry parent that ended with "I'm suing you!" In the afternoon, four-year-old Richie had a loud tantrum when asked to put his coat on before going outside, screaming and thrashing about. The teacher called a code blue, the internal signal for requesting help when a child is out of control. All in a day's work for Julie, handling upset people with challenging behaviors. First, Julie took six big breaths in sixty seconds. Then she handled each situation with similar techniques. She listened and she stayed calm, which deescalated the tension. She wrote notes after each incident and studied the Pyramid Model once again. She realized that it was not always possible to avoid random eruptions, but she could reduce them.

Parallels between Teaching and Leading

Teachers of young children know that behavior has a function. It's a way to communicate. Sometimes it is positive. Other times, it expresses anxiety, frustration, desire, or fear. The triggers tend to be in two categories: to obtain an object or attention, or to avoid a person or a task. As the leader of your organization, you have to address challenging behaviors coming from many directions—staff, children, and family members. There are similarities in the triggers. There are also similar strategies for dealing with these situations. Experts agree that the best way to deal with the effects of strong emotions is anticipating the triggers and using prevention as a tool to eliminate or minimize them.

Important Considerations

An early childhood education program is a relationship-based environment where children and adults interact closely for many hours. That makes it a cauldron for emotions. Young children are in the business of learning self-control, which means success is inconsistent. One minute toddlers are playing happily, and the next a hot dispute arises over a pink toy rabbit. Multiple reasons for stress come up throughout the day. They can be environmental, such as sound, light, temperature, or clutter. And they can be human, such as disappointments, high tension, or unfulfilled needs. Staff members can feel compassion burnout as they deal with the emotions of children and family members throughout the day. Family members have their own complex problems from family and professional situations, sometimes intermingled.

An individual's temperament affects their reaction to different situations. Everyone is on the continuum from low to high for intensity, persistence, activity, and adaptability. People who tend to be intense, active, and not adaptable are likely to have a louder response to a situation they don't want or like, be it an unfamiliar food, a change in schedule, or a new curriculum.

Coming from a high-context or low-context culture influences a person's style of behaviors too. In general, low-context cultures are in the Anglo-Saxon/Scandinavian groups, and high-context cultures are from the rest of the world. In regular conversations, a person from a high-context culture is focused on interpersonal relationships, facial expressions, body language, and personal information. A person from a low-context culture will be more focused on the topic at hand, directness, controlled feelings, and not much personal sharing. In tense interactions, these differences can be exacerbated, and the risk for misunderstanding increases.

Leaders cannot control the personal stress of the children, families, or staff, but they can control their own reaction to it. These practices work when confronted with an angry person:

During the incident, take the following steps:

- Pause. This slows down your reaction.

- Look at the other person with respect, even if you don't agree.

- Be compassionate. You may not understand, but you see their pain.

- Don't take it personally.

- Talk less. Listen as the other person talks.

- Do not match the other person's intensity.

- Don't look for an immediate solution. Your part is to deescalate the moment and plan to work on a common solution at a later time.

After the incident, reflect in the following ways:

- While the incident is fresh in your mind, write some notes. Jot down what the person was saying and what you think they wanted.

- Think about what could have prevented the situation.

- Analyze whether this was an isolated incident or repeated occurrence.

After your reflection, do the following:

- Remember that it is human to feel rattled by the anger and aggression of others.

- Take a walk, breathe, and relax your muscles.

- Be gentle with yourself and give yourself time to calm further.

- When you're ready, start thinking of solutions.

Practical Applications

Apply a Diversity and Equity Lens to Dealing with Challenging Behaviors of Children, Staff, and Families

The first recommendation of the NAEYC position statement on diversity and equity is to "build awareness and understanding of your culture, personal beliefs, values, and biases" (NAEYC 2019). This is particularly fitting for interpreting the behavior of others. Common human emotions of happiness, anger, fear, sadness, and surprise can be expressed very differently based on cultural norms or individual temperament. Our initial reaction may be to see a disobedient child, an irresponsible parent, or a difficult staff member. But consider how to relabel and reframe what we see: a high-intensity child learning to deal with the surprise of transitions; a busy parent learning to organize her family's bedtime schedule; an inexperienced teacher who fears asking for help. To gain extra insight and to practice understanding one another, consider professional development for you and the staff on cultural expectations surrounding behavior.

Strategies for Dealing with Challenging Behaviors of Children, Staff, and Families

1. Set high-level yet simple guidelines for positive behavior: respect yourself, respect others, respect the environment. The negative is also illustrative: do not hurt yourself, do not hurt others, do not hurt the environment. These rules are easy to apply universally to a variety of scenarios.

2. Be aware of cultural differences in the way adults express their strong feelings. Do not take the intensity of others personally, though it is reasonable to set limits so the display of intensity remains within the bounds of "respect yourself, respect others, and respect the environment."

3. Use the Pyramid Model (www.pyramidmodel.org) to plan for adults as well as children. The three levels of service fit well for managing both relationships and interactions. Universal strategies will be sufficient for about 75 percent of the group; additional support and attention will be needed for about 20 percent, which means that the leader must be more thoughtful and anticipate problems to minimize or control them; and extra support will be necessary for the last 5 percent, who need things to be more highly explained, managed, or clarified. Think about your staff and the families you serve and consider whether these basic calculations fit.

4. Organize an environment that reduces anxiety and stress for all. Some strategies include having consistent routines, giving positive affirmation, communicating expectations clearly, preparing carefully for changes, and employing a floating staff to be always available.

5. Watch the words you use. Avoid "always" or "never" when discussing a situation or problem, especially with someone who is angry or excitable.

6. Have a system to deal with a behavior crisis. If a teacher is overwhelmed by a child having an outburst, have a code blue system so the teacher can call the office and request relief to detach from the situation and come back refreshed. If a teacher needs a stress break, have a plan to staff a short-term replacement in their room. If a child acts up, add the floater to the classroom so the teacher can help the child calm down. If an adult acts up, remain polite, and try to get another person with you in the room or step into a public space.

7. Gather a list of mental health resources for adults. Contract with an Employee Assistance Program (EAP) to refer employees, and keep a list of local family assistance resources to refer family members.

8. Identify patterns to be able to anticipate emotional flare-ups. Tempers tend to be more unstable on Mondays, when everyone is making a transition from the weekend

to school or work, and on Fridays, when everyone is tired due to the intense activity of the center all week. Be on the alert for other situations more specific to your site that could make people irritable, for example, traffic jams due to road construction near the center or a holiday that disrupts normal routines.

9. Watch for late-afternoon stress. Studies have shown that cortisol (stress hormone) levels rise for children at the end of the day in child care, which influences the adults in the environment too. Plan accordingly—it is not the time to give negative feedback to an educator or to talk to a parent about a late payment.

10. Recognize the challenging behavior as a cry for help, not a personal attack. This will help you remain calm and look for solutions.

Reflection and Planning

As you finish reading this chapter, reflect on your practices in dealing with challenging behaviors of children, staff, and families.

1. Which ideas are familiar, and which are you already using in your daily work?

2. Which ideas would you like to explore further?

3. Choose one or two ideas that you would like to focus on, and use the SMART goal-setting formula to write down your goal:

Specific (What is the specific idea? Who will do it?)	
Measurable (How will you measure success?)	
Achievable (Is it possible to accomplish with the resources you have?)	
Relevant (Will it benefit your particular situation?)	
Time-bound (By when will it happen?)	

CHAPTER 12
LEADER WELLNESS

Robert received invaluable advice from his mentor when he became center director: take care of yourself and the job will actually feel easier. That seemed contradictory. Robert wasn't sure he would have time for himself. The previous director had quit, claiming burnout. Fortunately, the mentor coached Robert through the process. Together they put in place a wellness plan that addressed what they called "the pie of life." This pie of life divides into four slices: physical, social-emotional, mental, and spiritual. They joked that the categories were similar to the children's areas of development. Robert identified his priorities in each slice. In the physical slice, he recognized a need for a calming time every day after lunch, which happened to coincide well with naptime at the center. He closed his door and did ten minutes of a yoga routine with quiet music. He looked forward to this special moment for himself, after which he felt renewed and ready for the rest of the day.

Parallels between Teaching and Leading

Teachers are at risk for developing compassion fatigue when they interpret the needs of children and families as demands. They may start blaming the children for their problems or judging the families for not caring enough. They lose the capacity for empathy, feel tired all the time, and generally do not feel good about themselves or their jobs. As they become overwhelmed, they are not able to make rational professional decisions for lesson planning or behavior guidance, which adds to their personal distress. These are fairly common reactions that affect many other helping professions, including educational leadership. However, compassion fatigue is not inevitable when handled with common sense and practical wellness strategies, as in the story of Robert.

Important Considerations

Attrition is high for directors in early childhood programs. Yet all these leaders once aspired to a productive and rewarding career. The work is challenging and the supports are minimal (Institute of Medicine and National Research Council 2015). In most states, it is not necessary to have a director's license, and nowhere is it necessary to have a license as an owner of a center. Sometimes tensions rise when directors focus more on the quality of education while owners demonstrate more interest in the financial aspects. Whatever your situation, you are in company with other leaders who feel the weight of the field on their shoulders too.

A healthy family is not a family *without* stress but rather a family that learns to *handle* stress. The same concept applies to an organization. A well-functioning early childhood center is not a center without problems. Situations like having to redo the staffing schedule because of an absence, needing to order a new freezer when the old one breaks down, or dealing with an upset parent cause stress, but it is manageable stress when the organization is healthy. Leaders who take time for themselves to regroup and renew their energy have a better chance of seeing these events as problems to solve rather than experiencing them as personal assaults, feeling "Why me?" Then they are less likely to become exhausted and overwhelmed. A positive cycle even develops, as leaders are better able to think ahead and can begin to delegate some tasks and involve others in finding solutions.

Practical Applications

Apply a Diversity and Equity Lens to Leader Wellness

You are unique, and what works to keep you feeling balanced is personal and cultural. You have the right and the responsibility to find your preferred mode of self-care, as Robert does in the vignette. Focus on your body, mind, and spirit to be at your best. Rewarding and caring for yourself is not indulgence. In other caring professions, like nursing or medicine, self-care is considered an ethical imperative, and therefore a foundation of equity:

> *"I will attend to my own health, well-being, and abilities in order to provide care of the highest standard."*
> —Hippocratic Oath, Convention of Geneva

> *"The nurse owes the same duties to self as to others, including the responsibility to promote health and safety, preserve wholeness of character and integrity, maintain competence, and continue personal and professional growth."*
> —Nursing Code of Ethics

It is the proverbial recommendation that the flight attendant on the plane asks passengers to put on their own oxygen masks before putting them on the children, so they are better able to help in danger. Your good functioning is essential to keep up the high performance of your program, from the environment to the people.

Strategies for Leader Wellness

1. Delegate some tasks. You cannot do everything alone. Consider asking a parent committee to redesign the family lounge or ask senior staff to mentor junior members. In this way, you are a role model sending the message that everyone is working together.

2. Give yourself positive affirmations: "I am now calm and relaxed." "I enjoy eating my apple every day." "I exercise three times a week to keep my body and mind in good shape." "I did a good job this morning talking with Adam's mom. She left reassured." "Yes! I fixed the budget!"

3. Give positive affirmations to others. Acknowledging others in kind ways actually contributes to our own wellness. It is part of creating a caring community for all.

4. Join or create a support group of directors. In some areas, formal groups have been organized by the local AEYC or Child Care Associations. If none exist in your community, think of starting one by calling the local child care centers and inviting their leaders to join, in person or virtually. You will find an enthusiastic response from colleagues who feel isolated and welcome a chance to share their struggles and successes.

5. Organize and decorate your space to make it a pleasant place to be. You spend a lot of time at work. It is important that you feel comfortable, surrounded by objects and art that you enjoy.

6. Have a mirror in your office. This is not about vanity. It takes a calm brain to calm other brains. Just as the teacher acts as coregulator when a child is having a tantrum, when leaders model a calm presence though their tone, facial expression, and posture, others are less likely to react defensively and situations can be resolved quicker and better. A mirror allows you to take a quick look at your appearance, compose yourself with a confident smile, and get ready to face any challenge.

7. Practice the breathing exercise "6 x 60." The wellness movement recommends taking six breaths in sixty seconds. This is enough for a quick renewal of oxygen. This simple exercise reduces your heart rate, blood pressure, and cortisol levels. It is the first thing director Julie did in chapter 11 when dealing with challenging behaviors.

8. Practice mindfulness. Mindfulness is not an attitude but a practice. Start by visiting www.mindfulminutes.com.

9. Keep a journal. This allows you to express your thoughts and reactions in private. As you review it periodically, look for patterns that might lead to problem solving. It is also a method to document your successes.

10. Believe that you are enough. Like the good-enough parent or the good-enough teacher, there is a place for the good-enough leader. This is not a lowering of expectations. It is an acknowledgment that you are in progress. On the continuum of learning and performance, you are on the road.

Reflection and Planning

As you finish reading this chapter, reflect on how you practice wellness.

1. Which ideas are familiar, and which are you already using in your daily work?

2. Which ideas would you like to explore further?

3. Choose one or two ideas that you would like to focus on, and use the SMART goal-setting formula to write down your goal:

Specific (What is the specific idea? Who will do it?)	
Measurable (How will you measure success?)	
Achievable (Is it possible to accomplish with the resources you have?)	
Relevant (Will it benefit your particular situation?)	
Time-bound (By when will it happen?)	

CONCLUSION

The National Association for the Education of Young Children (NAEYC) *Developmentally Appropriate Practice* (DAP) position statement (2020) explains that quality education happens for children when educators "create a caring community of learners, enhance development and learning, plan an appropriate curriculum, and assess development and growth." These principles have a parallel for education leaders—create a caring community of workers, enhance professional competence, provide appropriate direction and resources, and assess skills and growth. It stands to reason that when education leaders treat educators in the way they expect them to treat children, everyone gains.

In the twenty-first century, we have seen a strong movement to improve the quality of early education. The focus began at the child level, considering what the children need to learn and how they can best learn it. As a result, early learning standards were developed, followed by many curricula and assessments. That led to more attention paid to teachers and their skills as core competencies were identified and various pedagogical models implemented.

But less attention has been paid to leadership in the field. A recent exploration of director hiring announcements on job search site Indeed.com gives one reason to pause. The duties and responsibilities described are very broad. They include items like "Must show evidence of emotional intelligence and ability which demonstrate the skill to show good judgment in handling crisis situations" and "Must be able to move quickly, bend, stoop, climb ladders and lift/carry up to fifty pounds on a regular and continuing basis." That points to unrealistic expectations that are often difficult to meet. At the same time, across the country the education and experience requirements for directors can be minimal (for example, high school diploma or GED and one year of experience in the classroom). Some programs prefer a master's degree but do not expect it to be in the field of early childhood education. Few states or higher education institutions offer degrees specific to early education leadership and management. The field is undersupported. We need advocacy at the local and national level to provide a stronger support to the courageous souls who aspire to be ECE directors and to those who are already doing the work.

In leadership workshops, when I ask audiences to describe the characteristics of a good toddler teacher, the words that come up are *flexible, sensitive, sense of humor, organize chaos, stamina, resourceful, caring.* When we look at the list together, there is a brief silence and a moment of realization as the parallel process becomes obvious. It's a relief not to look for magical solutions but to use the techniques you already know to lead your program. You run your program like you would run your classroom. You have a plan. You support and guide others. You assess quality and provide resources. You manage and solve problems. You create and promote conditions of trust, cooperation, well-being, growth, and self-esteem.

The benefits are all around. Your staff feels respected and motivated. The children and families are served by calm and skilled staff. They feel supported and valued. And you have the satisfaction that your leadership results in a well-organized and successful program. I wish you the very best as you continue your good work.

CHECKLIST

Below, I offer a checklist with the main themes of the book. It is one more tool to use for your personal planning. This checklist is intended as an overview of an education leader's job. It is a tool for self-assessment, not an evaluation instrument. All the items are important. Check the appropriate box on a scale of 1 (rarely) to 3 (frequently).

As a leader in early childhood education, I address these areas of my job . . .

	1 rarely	2 sometimes	3 frequently
As the leader . . .			
I share my vision for quality with staff, children, and families.			
I invite staff, children, and families to share their visions with me.			
I provide mirrors for my staff to see themselves.			
I provide windows for my staff to learn new ideas and practices.			
I practice my values of equity and diversity.			
Program Administration			
The program has a written strategic plan with specific goals.			
The strategic plan is evaluated yearly.			
The budget matches the program written goals.			
Records on finances, enrollment, and staffing are up to date.			
I manage the program with fairness (time, salaries, expectations).			

	1 rarely	2 sometimes	3 frequently
Time Management			
I stay aware of how I spend my time by doing periodic tracking.			
I have a clear system for open-door times that I communicate so staff and families know when I am available.			
I feel I can organize the flow of time most days.			
I alternate my schedule to be available at opening and closing times.			
Community of Workers			
Working conditions are good (fair pay, predictable schedule, reasonable flexibility).			
The environment is free of gossip.			
I smile and greet staff every day.			
I visit each classroom every day.			
I help educators feel connected to the field of early childhood education.			
I promote a climate of collaboration and sharing (materials, time, space).			
I have positive professional relationships with all staff.			
Professional Competence			
I have a plan for evaluating and supporting staff skills.			
The professional development plan is tailored to the group and to individuals.			
I give specific affirmations on performance.			
I encourage staff to persist even when the work is challenging.			

	1 rarely	2 sometimes	3 frequently
I give feedback when teaching or work is not going well.			
I scaffold staff skills.			
Children's Learning and Development			
I believe all children can learn, and I expect the same from staff.			
I demonstrate my beliefs that all children can learn by accommodating children's and families' needs and desires to be successful.			
I provide tools for educators to assess children's learning.			
I support educators in using data to improve practice.			
Communication			
A communication plan is in place (email, text, in person, large group, small group).			
I provide clear direction (e.g., behavior, curriculum, finances).			
I use plain language to talk about policies and early education.			
Listening and responding to one another is a cultural expectation of the program.			
Family Partnerships			
I have multiple systems of communication with families (in person, online, individual, group).			
I demonstrate a no-fault attitude toward families.			
I coach my staff in their roles as support to families.			
Physical Space			
I consider the physical space as the third teacher (ready for teaching, easily accessible materials, uncluttered, safe).			

	1 rarely	2 sometimes	3 frequently
The center has a maintenance plan.			
Responsibilities for the space are fairly managed (classrooms, public, multiuse, staff).			
Staff has access to clean and pleasant spaces for privacy and relaxation.			
Curriculum and Materials			
The curriculum addresses all areas of development.			
The curriculum reflects the values and goals of the program.			
I monitor the implementation of the curriculum.			
I provide resources and support to educators to implement the curriculum.			
Challenging Behaviors of Children, Staff, and Families			
I promote and demonstrate the prevention of challenging behaviors through communication, routines, and a calm environment.			
Our center has simple and direct behavior rules for adults (educators and families) and children.			
I use the Pyramid Model to address challenging behaviors of adults and children.			
I organize the physical and social environment to reduce stress.			
Leader Wellness			
I believe my wellness is important to the success of the center.			
I practice wellness habits that are culturally relevant to me.			
I find support for my professional skills as a leader.			
I know I'm good enough!			

REFERENCES

Barrera, Isaura, and Lucinda Kramer. 2017. *Skilled Dialogue: Authentic Communication and Collaboration across Diverse Perspectives.* Bloomington, IN: Balboa Press.

Bloom, Paula Jorde, Ann Hentschel, and Jill Bella. 2016. *A Great Place to Work: Creating a Healthy Organizational Climate*, 2nd ed. Lake Forest, IL: New Horizons.

Child Care Exchange. 2020. *The Art of Leadership Series.* Lincoln, NE: Exchange Press.

Derman-Sparks, Louise, and Julie Olsen Edwards. 2020. *Anti-Bias Education for Young Children and Ourselves*, 2nd ed. Washington, DC: NAEYC.

Derman-Sparks, Louise, Debbie LeeKeenan, and John Nimmo. 2015. *Leading Anti-Bias Early Childhood Programs: A Guide for Change.* Washington, DC: NAEYC and New York: Teachers College Press.

Forestieri, Marnie. 2021. *The Basics of Leading a Child-Care Business.* Lewisville, NC: Gryphon House.

Institute of Medicine and National Research Council. 2015. *Transforming the Workforce for Children Birth through Age 8: A Unifying Foundation.* Washington, DC: The National Academies Press.

Kaiser, Barbara, and Judy Sklar Rasminsky. 2021. *Addressing Challenging Behavior in Young Children: The Leader's Role.* Washington, DC: NAEYC.

Leekeenan, Debbie, and Iris Chin Ponte. 2018. *From Survive to Thrive: A Director's Guide for Leading an Early Childhood Program.* Washington, DC: NAEYC.

Masterson, Marie. 2022. *Refocusing Leadership Basics: Strengthening Staff Relationships.* McCormick Center for Early Childhood Leadership. https://mccormickcenter.nl.edu/library /strengthening-staff-relationships220104.

McCormick Center for Early Childhood Leadership. 2011. "Mentoring Directors as a Strategy to Improve Quality in Early Childhood Programs." Research notes. National Louis University.

Minnesota Departments of Education, Human Services, and Health. 2020. *Minnesota's Knowledge and Competency Framework for Early Childhood Professionals: Working with Preschool-Aged Children in Center and School Programs.* https://education.mn.gov/MDE/dse/early/highqualel/know.

NAEYC (National Association for the Education of Young Children). 2011. *Code of Ethical Conduct and Statement of Commitment.* NAEYC. www.naeyc.org/sites/default/files/globally-shared/downloads/PDFs/resources/position-statements/Ethics%20Position%20Statement2011_09202013update.pdf.

———. 2019. *Advancing Equity in Early Childhood Education.* Position statement. NAEYC. www.naeyc.org/resources/position-statements/equity-position.

———. 2020. *Developmentally Appropriate Practice (DAP).* Position statement. NAEYC. www.naeyc.org/sites/default/files/globally-shared/downloads/PDFs/resources/position-statements/dap-statement_0.pdf.

Nicholson, Julie, Priya Shimpi Driscoll, Julie Kurtz, Doménica Márquez, and LaWanda Wesley. 2020. *Culturally Responsive Self-Care Practices for Early Childhood Educators.* New York: Routledge.

Passe, Angèle Sancho. 2015. *Evaluating and Supporting Early Childhood Teachers.* St. Paul, MN: Redleaf Press.

———. 2020. *Creating Diversity-Rich Environments for Young Children.* St. Paul, MN: Redleaf Press.

Smith, Connie Jo. 2008. *Behavioral Challenges in Early Childhood Settings.* St. Paul, MN: Redleaf Press.

Talan, Teri N., and Paula Jorde Bloom. 2011. *Program Administration Scale (PAS): Measuring Early Childhood Leadership and Management,* 2nd ed. New York: Teachers College Press.

———. 2018. *Business Administration Scale for Family Child Care (BAS),* 2nd ed. New York: Teachers College Press.

RESOURCES

 Center for Inclusive Child Care
www.inclusivechildcare.org

 ChildCare Education Institute (CCIE) Director's Certificate
www.cceionline.com/directors-certificate

 First Children's Finance
www.firstchildrensfinance.org

 Head Start | ECLKC: Early Childhood Learning and Knowledge Center
https://eclkc.ohs.acf.hhs.gov

 McCormick Center for Early Childhood Leadership
https://mccormickcenter.nl.edu

 Mindful Minutes
www.mindfulminutes.com

National Association for the Education of Young Children (NAEYC)
www.naeyc.org

National Center for Pyramid Model Innovations (NCPMI)
https://challengingbehavior.cbcs.usf.edu

National Resource Center For Health and Safety In Child Care and Early
Education
https://nrckids.org

Pyramid Model Consortium
www.pyramidmodel.org

US Department of Health and Human Services Office of Child Care:
Resources for Child Care Providers
www.acf.hhs.gov/occ/providers